Some media extracts

Georgia Foster is the hypnotherapist charged with overcoming my tendency to over-drink. She says 'Let's be honest: nobody wants to live in a non-alcohol world. But it's about managing your alcohol, as opposed to letting it manage you. It's about not using drink as escapism from day-to-day problems.'
The Daily Telegraph

A female City Executive drank up to 90 units a week before finally seeking help and becoming one of the first British women to undergo therapy for binge drinking... 'It was a seven year binge that made me overweight, broke and sick. But I loved drinking and just didn't know when to stop. Georgia's theory was that I was drinking to escape the immense pressure I was putting myself under — I had to find another way, other than drinking, to silence my "Inner Critic", the voice telling me I was too fat or not pretty enough. The more I drank, the more confident I felt. I'd never really thought about why I was behaving like that, but working with Georgia made me realise how my insecurities were raging out of control. She focused on building my self-esteem and confronting my stress triggers so I no longer needed to comfort eat or binge drink. I started to make healthier choices simply because I gained respect for myself. The treatment was surprisingly easy and almost straight away I began drinking less and alternating wine with water.'
Glamour Magazine

Clinical Hypnotherapist, Georgia Foster, says about a third of her clients - mostly professionals and financial types - have alcohol related problems. "Drinking in the city is like a sport, although the consequences are swept under the carpet" she says. "Some of my clients can easily drink a bottle of wine at lunch and another after work. We all have an inner anxiety - I call it our inner critic - that tells

us we're not doing things well. Alcohol suppresses that and gives us confidence. The problem is the inner critic comes back stronger and fiercer, when you sober up, so you drink even more to bolster your confidence, and the cycle continues. It's all too easy to get into this sort of situation - it can happen to any of us - and unless you get help or sort it out, it can easily wreck your life."
The Sunday Times

Who is The Drink Less Mind for?
Anyone who feels their drinking is out of control. I don't mean alcoholics, but people who regularly drink more than they like, and are too shy to discuss it, but would like to retrain their mind to make it easier to cut down.
Why is it so hard to resist a drink?
We live in a 'cocktail culture', where there aren't many social options aside from bars and restaurants. We also drink more to open up to friends: alcohol becomes a form of therapy, to make it easier to discuss problems. Alcohol is relaxing, and we lead very stressful lives. But the unconscious mind does everything habitually, so there is a danger that you will come to associate stress relief with alcohol, and that nightly glass with dinner could, in time, turn into a bottle.
When is social drinking a problem?
When it becomes emotional and habitual. The process is twofold. First, you drink to alleviate stress, boredom or unhappiness; then your mind links this emotion to drinking, so you drink every time you feel this way.
Q & A, Psychologies Magazine

At 38, Polly has a high-powered marketing job in London. She's very social, very popular and very stressed. Like many women today, alcohol became her crutch; 'In my industry, it's used as relaxation, plus there's a lot of social pressure for girls to go out drinking. It's a massive problem,' she says. Although not an alcoholic, Polly confesses she had a problem saying no to the next glass, despite knowing the inevitable consequence. 'I would drink a load out with clients and colleagues, then have a massive hangover at work the next day.' She also drank on her own: 'My first thought when I came home was to unwind with a glass of wine. It was a tool to switch off the incessant blabber in my head.'

Polly's drink-to-cope pattern emerged when she consulted stress management expert and clinical hypnotherapist, Georgia Foster. For when they unpicked her behaviour, Polly was able to admit to herself that 'drinking in that way was not where I wanted to be.' She also realised that alcohol made her feel more stressed and tired, as well as fuzzy-headed. The key to finding the solution came when she understood that her subconscious reason for drinking was to make her feel more confident, both socially and professionally. In Georgia's experience, 'looking at life through a wine glass is most often an attempt to cover up fear and anxiety.'

Working through her problem has enabled Polly to say no to the next drink. 'I've stopped "people pleasing"; if I don't want another drink, I feel fine about having something non-alcoholic. I always thought I'd be more fun after a few drinks, but now I have alcohol-free days during the week. I know I'm a fun person to be around anyway.' She feels much calmer and able to cope with stress: 'I deal with things more pragmatically; rather than expecting to get something perfect, I think "Hey. I've given it my best."'

For everyone with what Georgia calls 'an over-drinking problem,' she has synthesised her treatment approach into a practical, easy-to-follow book called The Drink Less Mind which includes a relaxation/self hypnosis CD. 'Put it on when you get home, instead of having a drink; it really works.' says Polly.
You Magazine, The Mail on Sunday

'I've always liked a drink, but between my marriage breaking up and my father being very ill, I haven't had it easy recently and I have turned to alcohol for comfort. Every evening I intend to have a dry night but when I get home I think, "bugger it". When I am out with friends, I can drink two bottles of wine over the course of the evening - it's my treat. I hate myself for not having the willpower to stop because I know it's the lazy way of coping with my problems.'

I was to have 3 weeks of coaching with Georgia - one weekly session in person, and a personalised CD to listen to at night. I found the first session enlightening. Georgia asked me to keep a record of how much I drank to make me more conscious of my behaviour. Determined to be 'good', I put on Georgia's CD to help me relax when I got home rather than opening a bottle of wine and for the first time in years, I had an alcohol-free-day (AFD).

With a programme to stick to, it's not as hard as I imagined and I actually look forward to listening to the CD. I still have cravings for alcohol, but have just had five small glasses of wine in the past 10 days – a huge improvement. Week 3 I went out with friends and only drank half a bottle of wine, which for me is unheard of. I feel stronger and more accepting of my current situation, so there was less of an internal struggle and less of a void to fill with drink.
Psychologies Magazine

'Whether I was happy, sad, exhausted or stressed, I'd open a bottle of red wine." she says. 'When I was on maternity leave the first thing I did when my husband got home from work was have a glass of wine. It made me feel like an adult again after spending all day with the children. Stopping work to have kids affected my confidence. I felt less interesting as I didn't have much to talk about other than my babies.' Jo had successfully stopped smoking with Georgia, so decided to use hypnotherapy to cut back on her drinking. 'I still enjoy a drink or to two several times a week and if I got out I will indulge. The difference is I can control it now.'
In The Know magazine

The Drink Less Mind™

The **truth** behind overdrinking

Acknowledgements

Mum, thank you so much for your fabulous editing. This book would not exist without your knowledge and understanding about my special work. I love you eternally.

Thank you so much to my incredible supportive partner Ian. You are the love of my life. Thank you also for giving us our beautiful triplet sons, Ollie, Finn and Hugh.

Infinite kisses and hugs to my loving father Richard and my beautiful sister Virginia.

To Fi, thanks for your very special gift to help this book to come to fruition. Joy, thanks for your beautiful home to write in. Gerald, thanks for helping me out. Kath, thanks for the laughter in challenging moments.

To my very special Sue Blake, you have truly been an 'earth angel' who now resides in heaven. Oh how I miss you!

Simon, thanks for your clever drawings in the book, I love them!

Thanks to all my clients and workshop participants for your invaluable input.

About the Author

Georgia Foster has been working as a Clinical Hypnotherapist and Voice Dialogue Trainer since 1995 in London, United Kingdom. Originally from Melbourne, Australia, her personal experience with low esteem, alcohol and food issues led to years of self exploration to find answers. This book represents her successful work with thousands of people.

Georgia previously wrote The Weight Less Mind and co- wrote Slim By Suggestion TM (Thorsons, 2001).

Other books include The Stress Less Mind, The 4 Secrets of Amazing Sex and her highly successful on-line program www.howtodrinkless.com.

Georgia has been featured in the press in the UK and Australia regularly from breakfast TV, Sky News to The Sunday Times, Good Housekeeping to Psychologies magazine and more. She is regularly quoted for her unique approach and highly successful approach to drinking less.

Georgia Foster asserts the moral right to be identified as the author of this work

The Drink Less Mind™ is a trademark of Georgia Foster Limited

© Georgia Foster 2005

Reprint 2005, 2006, 2007, 2008

Typeset by Steve Verity
www.fever-design.co.uk

Published by Georgia Foster Publishing
www.georgiafoster.com

Proofread by Kelly Owen, www.ultimateproof.co.uk

Music composed by Nick Crofts

CD produced by Sound Recording Technology, 01480 461 880

ISBN 1 903607 74 4

A catalogue record for this book is available from the British Library

Printed and bound in Great Britain by Berforts Information Press, Kings Lynn, Norfolk

Contents

Introduction

This book is to help us understand the ups and downs of life through our drinking ability: by this, I mean the 'why?', and the 'how?'

First of all, why do we drink? Do we drink to relax or socialise or do we drink because we feel an emotional tie to the comfort a drink provides for us? Is drinking a form of escape?

Life will always have its ups and downs – this is an unavoidable fact and our consumption of alcohol can follow the same pattern. It is natural during certain times or events in our life to use alcohol for different purposes, for example, brandy is quite often used for shock and champagne used in celebration. Tied into this equation is our mind, for our mind's reaction to alcohol has a huge bearing on the 'why?' and 'how?' of our drinking behaviour.

Often our silent thoughts or 'mind chatter' can be extremely vocal, telling us how we 'should' be: that we 'should' eat less, drink less or be more proactive in our life. These 'should do's' keep replaying in our minds incessantly until they become a vicious cycle, and to quiet them we often suppress them in some form or another. Suppressing the 'should do's' for some people can take place either with food, or drugs, or sometimes sleep, and for others it is with the use of alcohol.

This book will be of interest to those who choose alcohol to deal with the difficulties of life and who regularly drink more than they feel they would like to or should. There are many men and women from all walks of life such as corporate, legal, sales and of course mums and dads who recognise that their relationship with alcohol has been or is creating more stress in their lives instead of relieving it.

Alcohol, on one level, aids stress management and relaxation, but on another level it can become a mind-numbing drug used (and often abused) to avoid and suppress certain situations in life.

Before we go any further, I feel the need to tell you that I am not condemning the sale or consumption of alcohol: rather, I am suggesting that you may wish to look at 'how' and 'why' you and your alcohol habits live together. And for this purpose, I suggest you use this book as an aid to gain insight through using it as a journal. This process will help you to understand the attractive seduction of alcohol and how it can either enhance our enjoyment of life or wreak havoc, and whether you choose to use alcohol or alcohol uses you.

What's wrong with drinking too much?

Alcohol has always been part of our lives, from ancient times through to this present day. Red wine is used in some Christian churches as a symbol of Christ's blood, while in other religions it is referred to as 'the demon drink'.

Red wine also has valuable health-giving properties which the medical and other health professionals now recognise as being beneficial, therefore it is often advised that certain men or women consume one or two glasses with an evening meal to assist in maintaining healthier blood.

Alcohol benefits many of us socially, too: as a relaxant it also helps us gain confidence, make new friends or embark on new relationships; however, it can have the very opposite effect if a man or woman begins to rely on having a drink to help them for emotional reasons.

Alcohol usage has the potential to become a habit in a short space of time and when this happens, a person creates for themselves various anxieties, low self-worth and the inability to make healthy decisions in life – this, therefore, prevents a person from moving forward. The long-term mis-use of alcohol causes physical, mental and emotional damage, which is indeed is very concerning.

Gillian Hamer, an international nutritionist and my work colleague, explains the effects of alcohol on the body in chapter 5: You and Your Liver. Gillian's extensive knowledge helps us understand the damage done to our bodies when we mis-use alcohol, and how we can assist our bodies in their return to well-being through health drinks and supplements. Contained also is advice to help the liver cope before an occasional big night out; however, it is important to remember these tips are for *before* that big night out and *occasional* use, not maintenance.

We will also have fun covering the different emotional aspects of 'how' and 'why' we drink, and the effects of the interconnection between the mind and the liver and how we disconnect the two through Inner Body Dialogue.

The Drink Less Mind also contains truthful (and perhaps close to the bone) case studies; these will help you recognise that you are not alone in your concerns about how much you may be drinking and why. The issues will range from anxiety, insomnia and sexual problems through to weight loss and finances. The underpinning of these issues is learned dependence on alcohol due to lack of self-worth and self-esteem and is often a cry for help.

The desire to cope better in life situations means that we often reach for alcohol to use as a coping mechanism, a confidence-boosting crutch. While this may work short-term, the long term consequences of it can be far reaching and often end in disaster. Using alcohol to cope with life takes its toll on the mind and body creating long-term stress, ill health and anxiety, not to mention its effects on your relationships, performance at work, your sex drive and general outlook on life.

The Drink Less Mind is a culmination of my 11 years as a self-esteem therapist working with men and women who have chosen to recognise that they don't want to drink as much and they want to get out of the rut of habitual drinking, because it is having a negative effect on their lives. Working with these courageous people is indeed rewarding, for they soon discover that beneath their fear and anxiety they have been hiding all their warmth, cleverness, strength, vitality, truth and kindness. As a result, after hypnosis, they feel released and free to enjoy life and get on with living a more sober life because now they know they can have a drink and enjoy it without going to excess.

For many people the sheer fact that they sought help, perhaps after years of putting it off, is enough for them to feel recharged and renew their zest for living. Procrastination on any issue in life holds us back. Getting real about your alcohol dependency will liberate you and enable you to take a close upfront and personal look at the rest of your life, without looking at it through the bottom of a glass.

Our shadow follows us wherever we go and even though the sun does go down every night, it rises the following morning with or without a hangover, a furry tongue, stale breath and less money in our purse or wallet.

"LOOK, THEY'VE GOT A NEW COCKTAIL CALLED 'AFTER WORK SHAG'."

Chapter 1

Life Through Rose-Coloured Claret

Our cultural heritage is to raise a glass and enjoy a drink for it is socially acceptable. Like many people, I enjoy nothing better than having a few glasses of wine with family and friends. There are also some evenings when having a glass of wine at the end of the day represents for me 'tools down and no more work for the day'; however, this does not mean I reach consistently for that pint of beer or glass of wine to unwind after work, for there are other ways to switch off your mind and relax.

Instead of looking at life continually through the blur of rose-coloured claret, whisky, bourbon or beer to hide your fears and anxieties, I propose that there is an enjoyable, rewarding and positive alternative that can break your reliance on alcohol so you can live life to your fullest potential.

The Drinking Society

The drinking patterns of society differ around the world as each country has its own licensing laws, and even different states within these countries may have their own licensed hours.

The After-Hours Office Drink Scene

Regardless of the country in which they live, men and women around the world gather after hours to relax and unwind after a hard day or week's work. Carefully constructed façades fall away as the beer or wine flows, the tongue loosens and individuals vent their emotions or reveal hidden truths about their lives. There is much to be revealed about another person's life when the booze is at hand, for discretion falls by the wayside and the listener learns more than he or she needs or wants to know.

The after-hours drink scene is often the place for after-hours office flirtations. It is the place where people who maliciously enjoy gossiping collect their information to talk about over coffee the next day. The gossip flies around the work place as to who tried to kiss who or who wanted to kiss who and who did or didn't kiss who!

The next day, when either the man or woman who unintentionally divulged hidden truths about their life or flirted with a co-worker enters their place of work, they feel distressed, embarrassed and uncomfortable about how they behaved the night before.

The Magic Elixir

There are times when we drink in the belief that this 'magic elixir' will supply us with self-confidence, sexual liberation, fun, creativity and a holiday from life's day to day problems. And, under certain circumstances, it does help to create an ambience of fun, love and peace; however, it can also create the exact opposite effect when we mistakenly use alcohol as the only way to experience these feelings in our life, for then we are searching endlessly for the illusion and not enjoying and living in the present, and so life-affirming moments and experiences pass us by as we befuddle our brain and miss out on living.

Discovering why your drinking patterns continually place you under stress will help you to gain conscious recognition of why you unconsciously drink, and you will gain understanding and insight into how and why these patterns have occurred. You will learn how to alter and update your drinking patterns with methods which you will enjoy, while working with the deeper part of your mind. This is when you can start to re-educate your mind to create new coping strategies that support, rather than work against, your emotional and physical health and well-being. The enclosed CD is part of this re-education and will be explained in more detail in chapter 3.

Stress Equals Alcohol

Stress comes in many mysterious guises, ranging from insomnia to all forms of psychosomatic symptoms through to depression. When Kate walked into the room it was obvious that she was extremely tense as her physical body was in gridlock. When seated, much to her embarrassment, she burst into tears; something she had promised herself she wouldn't do. This is not an uncommon reaction after making the brave decision to seek therapeutic advice. Crying is a simple, honest step toward releasing emotions.

Handing her my 'happy' tissues, I explained that tears are a natural form of stress relief, to which Kate sobbingly replied, "I feel stressed all the time. To the outside world my life is pretty good but I feel like I am continually running against time all the time. My boss is difficult, which makes me anxious – I always feel like I'm in trouble. I don't sleep well and I feel as if I am always dragging my feet. I don't even have the energy to go to the gym or do anything apart from work. On the weekend I party really hard and then dread the thought of Monday."

When I asked Kate what she did at the end of her working day, she answered that to de-stress she would either go out with work colleagues for a few drinks or go home and slump on the sofa with her flatmate, drink some wine and order in food. Kate then went on to say, "I like my social life. I have loads of fun and my flatmate is great company but I think we can drink too much. I often feel hung over from too much wine but once we get on a roll it eases the stress. The worst thing is, I sleep well for the first few hours and then have a fitful sleep because I become tense and worried about work the next day, not to mention the hangover. I feel overwhelmed sometimes by the fear that I am not good enough at my job and that I am going to be found out. I guess my boss keeps me on my toes."

My concern for Kate was not 'how' much Kate drank but the reasons behind 'why' she drank, for I knew that by gaining insight into 'why', then the 'how' of her drinking pattern would decrease. Kate was not giving herself enough time to process the stress at the end of her working day. In Kate's mind, alcohol had become a stress management tool and so to relieve the stress she reached for a bottle of wine, and the following morning she experienced anxiety, self-doubt and anger as well as mental and physical exhaustion.

Kate's mind had got her into a drinking rut by creating an emotional routine of habitual drinking, in the mistaken belief that this helped her cope with life. Kate loved the work she did but her boss was a bully and she felt like she was walking on eggshells in the office. Kate was placed in a stressful working situation and she was unable to see that her heavy drinking created more stress, as it clouded her judgement and depleted her confidence, which led to a loss of belief in herself.

In just over a month of working with Kate, she was able to assess for herself that her drinking was preventing her from moving on with her life. She gained in confidence which enabled her to make an appointment to talk with her boss. She prepared herself beforehand and during the meeting explained that she loved her work and asked if there was any other way that she could help him out. Her boss was taken by surprise and relieved to find out that she loved her job, as he could not understand why she had been so unhappy. Through opening the doors of communication the bullying boss became more amicable and Kate began to look forward to Mondays once again. Within weeks, Kate moved out of her drinking cycle and was able to enjoy alcohol-free evenings. Through listening to her CD, Kate's life became more harmonious and she moved from gulping wine by the bottle to savouring the taste of a glass or two.

Life is Celebration

We celebrate life as we raise our glasses and toast the major events in our lives. Champagne is a symbol of celebrating positive moments in life: this is evident from the number of greetings cards which feature a bottle, a popping cork or a glass. Years ago, new mothers were advised by doctors to drink champagne if they were suffering from mild 'after baby blues'. Champagne is used in novels, films, plays and television to convey the art of seduction as well as celebration. It symbolises the good things in life such as health, wealth and happiness.

Brandy is used to assist a person in recovery when they have suffered a sudden shock or been involved in an accident. For centuries, the Benedictine Monks were renowned throughout the world for their fine alcohol and Benedictine is still popular to this day.

Alcohol has been an important part of our lives from before biblical times through to the present moment and will continue to be in the years ahead. And 'because of' not 'in spite of', we need to consume it wisely so we gain the benefits of this wonderful beverage and enjoy life to the full.

Freeing yourself from your mind's mistaken equation that you will only be able to cope if you have that habitual drink is a new learning concept and it can be a scary prospect, for it is like living without that crutch. However, you will learn and understand from reading this book and listening to the CD how to throw away that crutch so you can walk unencumbered and experience the freedom of living in new found harmony with yourself and others. The process in this book will assist you in taking the necessary steps to liberate you from your drinking pattern.

Reaching for that much-needed drink is not liberating you: in fact, it is imprisoning you so you cannot experience the freedom of living in self-harmony; instead, you exist in a self-imposed world of anxiety, depression and pain.

This approach is a new way of celebrating 'you' without alcohol through opening the doors of your self-imposed alcohol prison and stepping into freedom. In doing this, you will re-discover the person you believed you had lost, who lives deep inside you and is fresh, funny, intelligent and confident. This is the person you mistakenly believed could be found in the next gin and tonic.

We all have anxieties and concerns and this is why I would like to share some examples and home truths with you, to provide you with the conscious and unconscious tools to assist you to deal with these stresses and anxieties without alcohol. In this book you will learn to understand how to salute the real inner you: the person who is fun, smart, confident and definitely worth celebrating!

The Radio Crazy Syndrome

You may not have consciously thought about how you actually talk to yourself until you read this book; however, the fact is we all continually talk to ourselves all the time. Talking to ourselves is a normal activity and at times the voice is positive; however, when the talk is negative (which it often is) then it is detrimental to our self-esteem and self-belief. To the outside world our inner chatter is silent, but internally how we talk to ourselves can be extremely abusive and violent. I call this syndrome 'Radio Crazy', as it goes on and on and on and in desperation we try to turn the volume down or silence it or change the station through drinking too much.

The following is a list of questions that are representative of the Radio Crazy thoughts that continuously run through many of our minds:

- Do you wake up in the morning feeling anxious because the first thing you think about is what you said last night after a few drinks?
- Are you surprised that no matter how busy you are, you can't wait to finish work and have a drink?
- Do you feel isolated from other people when you don't drink?
- Do certain situations or people trigger you to binge drink?
- Do you recognise how you are affected by stress?
- Do you feel as if you are going mad sometimes because you can't get your head around a problem and a drink helps clear your mind?
- Do you feel anxious eating with people without having a drink?
- Do you enjoy drinking on your own?
- Do you get annoyed with other people who don't drink when you want to?
- Do you drink to help you in certain situations?
- Do you drink to help you deal with confrontation?
- Do you procrastinate about life and put things off by drinking?
- Do you avoid sexual contact until you have had a drink?
- Do you have drinking buddies who encourage you to over-drink when you don't want to?
- Do you drink alcohol to alleviate emotional pain on a regular basis?

If you answered 'yes' to any or all of these questions, then this demonstrates how much you have tuned into your Radio Crazy and it has become a listening habit. Our inner conversations instruct us as to 'how' we deal with life and issue consistent statements to us such as the following: "He thinks you're boring – have another drink to cope." or: "Why can they have just one drink to relax and enjoy themselves when you need at least three or more?" or: "To get through this situation you'll need a drink." This form of negative self-talk becomes programmed into the minds of many men and women and to dull this negative talk they choose to drink.

Joe's Radio Crazy

A few years ago, 32-year-old Joe came to see me about his issue with weight. Joe worked as an IT consultant in one of the big investment banks in the business district of London. He was worried that he was gaining weight, for he was getting bigger and bigger by the week. His co-workers had started making fun of him, which only helped to exacerbate his weight gain, and Joe was losing his self-esteem. A shy man by nature, Joe had attended a boys' private school and he felt that he was never very popular and, as a result of this, he had kept pretty much to himself.

As Joe and I talked, I learned that when he had finished school and went to university he discovered beer, and not just beer but barrels of the stuff. Joe noticed that in the process of his beer-drinking he was becoming popular, for he became known for 'how' he could consume his beer and still keep standing – an heroic feat in the eyes of fellow students, and so Joe became a bit of a hero. This worked well at university; however, once he was out in the real working world, Joe discovered that his demanding desk job give him little personal time. His life became a routine of going to the pub, grabbing a curry to eat and then bed – as a consequence of this lifestyle his weight spiralled out of control.

Joe was out most nights drinking with his work colleagues and the nights he didn't drink, he stayed at home. He said, "I couldn't imagine going out after work and not drinking – it would be too stressful." I asked him why it would be stressful and he responded, "While at work it's okay to talk about certain things, but once in the pub there is more pressure to be entertaining and the thought of trying to do this sober just isn't comfortable."

Joe's weight issues were lifestyle related, but most importantly his mind had educated him emotionally as he believed that his move from an introverted shy child to a popular adult was aided by his drinking. He mistakenly believed his drinking had provided the basis for his social confidence. In order for Joe to lose weight, it wasn't just about drinking less and eating healthier food: it was about re-educating his mind that he had the ability to be confident without alcohol. For the fact was, if he could be confident with a few pints under his belt, it meant he had the ability to be popular without drinking, but the Radio Crazy in his head when he was sober kept repeatedly telling him he was boring, which was far from the truth.

Joe was relieved when he came to understand that his lifestyle pattern was a result of the Radio Crazy voice of his childhood which prevented him, when sober, from accessing his confident part and moving forward. Joe listened to his CD and his drinking and eating patterns altered so that he no longer over-drank or over-ate.

Radio Crazy talk has become an emotional habit for many men and women who, just like Joe, falsely believe their self-confidence only surfaces when consuming that much needed drink. When in reality the confident person is being suppressed, buried deep inside through the abuse of alcohol. It may sound strange, but your mind has trained itself through the years to think this way. In fact, your mind keeps telling you this is how you deal with life – that alcohol equals confidence and so, just like Joe, you drown the confident you in alcohol.

Through training in Voice Dialogue and hypnotherapy, I realised that every person can break free of this self-destructive mode by retraining the mind. Through this book and CD you will learn how Radio Crazy is a trained habit, a habit you can free yourself from as you learn how to deal with it.

Self Improvement

Over the course of reading this book and listening to the CD, you will start to notice that you are no longer berating yourself as much and that you have more peace in your mind and body. As your self-esteem starts improving, so too will your attitude towards alcohol. Physically, you will start to feel relief as you recognise and release the anxiety and self-doubt, because emotionally you will lose the need to use alcohol as a social, sexual, emotional crutch.

Soon your Radio Crazy will start to become a thing of the past. Later in the book we will discuss more about this; however, for now, just trust that the process of change is your right. Every one of us has the right to like ourselves, including you! It may be difficult for you to imagine, but once you start to believe in your own sober, confident you, the more confident you will become.

Your Positive Radio Station

The previously asked questions are made up of some of the most common Radio Crazy statements. Now think about what it would be like if you could change these negative comments into positive ones, for it can be done, for these comments relate to a state of mind and you can retrain your mind and body to be healthy and happy with yourself. Coping with life and enjoying it without over-drinking is a positive habit you can learn.

The tools contained in this book will consciously and unconsciously help you to tune in and experience in your mind a wonderful, supportive, relaxing radio station. You learn how to increase the positive volume until it becomes a healthy, harmonious habit within you.

The following statements are the opposite of the previous questions:

- I wake up in the morning and feel good about last night. I know that what I said and did is okay and I don't need to beat myself up.
- No matter how busy I am, I value that downing my work tools doesn't mean that I have to drink to relax. I now choose other situations that enhance my personal life.
- I am enjoying being able to go out and not having to drink all the time. It is refreshing to know that I can remember conversations and have met some interesting people.
- When I am with my boss even though he likes to drink I now feel confident to say 'no' if I choose.
- I value that my stress levels can be high sometimes and now that I recognise the signs I deal with stress more appropriately, rather

than over- drinking, and I feel proud of myself.

- When things get too much in my head I take time out by going for a walk or sitting quietly. It gives me the space to realise what I can change and what I can't.
- I enjoy going out with people and having a conversation sober. It is liberating.
- I now enjoy having a drink on my own without guilt. If I want to enjoy a drink, I do, but now I value my time on my own and enjoy my own company without feeling alone and drinking too much.
- If people don't want to drink that is fine. I like the fact that people make their own choices just as I do.
- I recognise that I need to address certain situations sober. I practise in my mind first what I need to do, so that I don't need that drink for false courage.
- I know that I am the only person who can discuss my problems with the right person, and saying things sober means I have the courage to discuss things seriously and that I do mean business.
- When I have a desire to do something without alcohol, I write it down, so that I can see clearly what I want to achieve.
- Each day I do something that supports this desire so that I don't have to listen to my Radio Crazy.
- I love making love sober. I feel the intensity and enjoy the sensations of being intimate: this increases my confidence as a sexual being.
- I now do not socialise as much with people who want to drink excessively when I don't.
- I recognise that emotionally there are things in my past that cause me pain. I am now addressing this pain rather than suppressing it with alcohol.

In Chapter 3: The Software of Your Mind, you will discover that the above statements can be yours. There will be many other statements you would like to include: you can enlarge this list if you choose so they become part of your everyday life statements that support your true desire to like yourself, whether you choose to drink in a given situation or not. We will explore more statements as we move along.

The CD in the Back of the Book

By the end of chapter 3, you will be ready to listen to track 1 of the CD. Chapter 3 explains in great detail the power of your mind and its incredible ability to change your relationship with yourself and alcohol. This chapter will also alleviate any misconceptions you may have about the safety of hypnosis. Hypnosis is a positive, powerful tool which helps people move forward and take positive action with life.

The most wonderful gifts you can give to yourself are clarity, health and happiness. Sometimes it means drinking and sometimes it doesn't. The CD in the back of the book will help aid those moments when alcohol isn't supporting your coping mechanisms. The CD will help you relax while drifting into a lovely space where you can have time out to re-evaluate what is right for you and who is right for you, and whether the situation you find yourself in is right for you.

The use of the CD is an important, pleasant and relaxing part of your emotional exercise as it will assist you in placing people, events and situations into perspective.

Get ready to take time out for yourself and experience the wonderful sensations of gaining self-worth through deep relaxation emotionally and physically, and enjoy it!.

Something to Think About – The AFD

I would like to introduce you to the AFD. It stands for an Alcohol-Free Day where you commit to 24 hours free from consuming alcohol. For some of you this may seem daunting, for others, easy. Once again, this book is not about berating you and your drinking patterns; rather, it is about seeing these patterns with the benefits of a clear mind and healthier body and this means drinking less and sometimes not at all.

Many clients tell me they drink every day, whether it is a spirit drink when they get in from work or sharing a bottle of wine with a partner over dinner. This is both respectable and acceptable, but perhaps sometimes you do not feel like indulging in your customary drink and you face a dilemma of making the decision of "should I, shouldn't I have a drink tonight?". The prospect of an AFD may seem a bit of a challenge, but during the process of reading this book and listening to the CD, an AFD will become more comfortable emotionally, and eventually, acceptable.

AFDs are a great way of getting in touch with the 'real' you, and it is a wonderful way to take time out for your mind and body. I will be covering more about AFDs later, but for now all you need to do is just think about the concept. Through purchasing The Drink Less Mind you have begun to explore the choices you have in life, and one is to gain positive benefits for your mind and body. An AFD is a fabulous way to look at your life and gain a healthy perspective of where you are now, where you are going and where you deserve to be.

"MY LIFE DOESN'T UNDERSTAND ME".

Chapter 2

Inner Dialogue

Inner Dialogue is a wonderful and powerful tool which gives us the opportunity to recognise the conversations we all have with ourselves that trigger the desire to drink too much.

Inner Dialogue goes deeper into the Radio Crazy Syndrome of how we talk to ourselves internally. To the outside world this Inner Dialogue is invisible as we have become experts at hiding this internal chatter, and so we are both thankful and relieved that people cannot read our minds! However, how we talk to ourselves is often of great disservice to our emotional well-being. Many people are relieved when they discover that everyone has an Inner Dialogue – it's not just you!

We are all made up of many parts or sub-personalities. These parts originally developed in the software of our minds unconsciously when we were very young: in fact, when we were babies. They developed at this early stage of our life to both protect and help us deal with life situations, and from there they became habitual. For example, if you look at the dynamics of your family's make-up, whether you were one of two or more siblings or an only child, you may recognise, perhaps, that you were the child who kept the peace in the family home, or maybe you were the gregarious or mischievous child who could get away with a lot. Either way, somewhere from infancy, your mind decided that the best way of being loved was to develop certain personality traits. The aim of these personalities was protection against your feelings and being vulnerable. This process may have worked well for many years, until you reach the age where you have to go out into the 'big' world, and it is then that you realise that sometimes these personality traits are a hindrance rather than a help to you, and so you might use alcohol as a way to feel safe.

Case Study – Anne

The family environment Anne grew up in was one that supported well-behaved children, and by the time Anne came to see me at the age of 39, she was one stressed-out person.

Within a few minutes of our meeting, Anne expressed that she was not comfortable admitting that she had issues. The 'Good Child' syndrome develops in men and women who have learnt as children to keep the peace, and the result is that they do not feel comfortable revealing and discussing their problems. Anne had spent her entire life working to make sure everything was okay whether at work or home, and to relieve her stress and the never-ending self-imposed pressure, she ate and drank too much.

The reason why Anne came to see me was because she had recently been diagnosed with diabetes. The doctor told her that she had to cut down on her sugar intake, which obviously included alcohol.

Anne and her husband were both big drinkers and were also very sociable people. They were always out and about and also entertained a lot at home.

Anne was concerned about how she was going to manage cutting back on alcohol when it was such a big part of her life. She relied on it. She said that she felt deep down that cutting back on her drinking would affect her relationship with her husband and her friends. When I asked her why, she answered, "If I cut back on my drinking, I won't be as keen to socialise and play host to our guests. I find without a drink it's too stressful. I'm quite shy by nature." What was apparent to me was that Anne played the 'Good Child' extremely well by looking after everybody else, and to accomplish this she did her best to ensure that everything flowed as peacefully as possible both socially and at home: the thought of having to carry on while being sober was causing her great anxiety.

Throughout the years, as Anne was growing up, she learned that by behaving as the good, shy daughter she received praise and rewards, so she spoke only when spoken to. To put it simply, Anne as a child had buried her internal voice of expressing what she felt and wanted, for this had made her feel wanted and while this had worked well for her in the past, unfortunately this old behaviour pattern was now detrimental to her. The 'Good Child' behaviour was no longer acceptable, as it was causing Anne serious health problems.

Developing the Healthy Confident Part

In order for Anne to drink less, it wasn't going to just be a matter of cutting back on alcohol: it was a matter of her understanding how to address her anxieties as a sober person. Anne was no longer a child and she needed to free her mind from its habitual training of only speaking when spoken to.

Life without alcohol or drinking less would be difficult for Anne and she realised this, so I explained to her how important it was for her to develop her inner Healthy Confident Part, and that this inner part had been silenced as a child as speaking up would have caused conflict with her parents.

Anne (just like everybody else) has the right to like her own self and feel confident when sober. In her mind, Anne saw sobriety as an unsafe experience as she felt she needed that drink to feel confident. I explained to Anne that what we needed to do was educate and free her mind so she would lose her anxiety and feel confident and at ease socially while drinking less.

To assist Anne, I suggested the Baby Step programme which is doing one small thing to enhance her confidence without alcohol being involved. Anne did struggle with this at first; however, eventually she discovered that she could go out for lunch with a 'safe' friend and not drink.

Just this one step meant her mind was already experiencing safety and sobriety in an environmental experience where she had previously used alcohol as a crutch. I explained to Anne that just one step is the beginning to freedom and connection with her Healthy Confident Part. I assured her that the process would become more and more comfortable and give her choices over her drinking patterns, and that in a short period of time she would become very comfortable with her new choices.

Anne came back after the first week grinning from ear to ear. She had been listening to her CD regularly and had lunched with her friend, which proved to be a very positive experience. Each week we set a new task that supported Anne's Healthy Confident Part and, as a consequence, her blood sugar level dropped plus she felt more energised, and she also discovered that socialising without alcohol increased her self-confidence and enhanced her relationship with her husband, both communicatively and sexually.

Decisions

Inner Dialogue is about breaking down and understanding the inner conversations we all have with ourselves. It could be likened to you being the gardener of your own mind. The positive dialogue which you planted through the years are the flowers, and the negative dialogue are the weeds. And so it is important for every one of us to discover, recognise and listen to the positive voice/parts we have created throughout life's journey, the ones which support us in our adult life, as well as discovering and recognising the negative voice/parts that are non-supportive and lead to ill health.

This process is a fun and enlightening experience, for as you begin to explore and discover your Inner Dialogue you will find yourself able to make decisions about what is right for you now. You will discover what is relevant to the way you choose to live your life, rather than living in a pattern of non-productive behaviour carried forward from your past years which prevent you from enjoying life.

Anne had fun discovering, listening and learning how to access her Healthy Confident Part and now she happily attends social gatherings and family occasions and achieves intimacy without over-drinking. Anne recognised that her 'Good Child' part, which had worked well for her as a child, was not what she needed in certain situations as an adult, as it was this part that was holding her back and the cause of her over-drinking.

We all have many different parts which are similar to those of other people, and this is why we identify with those who create similar experiences to our own. When our Inner Dialogue is negative, it hinders our self-belief: this is why we often use alcohol to help us deal with the insecurities we may have.

As you are reading these words you may understandably feel daunted; however, do not be, for the next few chapters will help you attain a sense of freedom as you gain insight and understanding into how these inner voices/parts work, for we all carry them inside us. These have come into place with good intentions, but through the years in the software of your mind you have trained these inner voices/parts to work against you and your best made plans.

The Inner Critic

I am now going to introduce the part that I spend most of my client time with: this is the part that underpins the suppression of our desires in life, and one of the ways it suppresses our desire is through over-drinking. This voice/part is called the Inner Critic.

The following are examples of the types of Inner Critic comments that I hear from my clients:

- I feel I am not coping well with my life.
- I can't find the strength to change jobs.
- Everybody else seems to cope better with their lives.
- I know I need to lose weight but I just can't find the motivation.
- I am angry at the world.
- Life is unfair.
- Nothing ever seems to go right in my life.
- What's the point in trying to improve my life, it never lasts anyway.
- I'm not good enough.
- I'm a hopeless case.
- If people really knew me they wouldn't like me.

Does This Sound Familiar?

I could write a whole book on these comments alone, for these are just some that come from most clients when we start to work together. To the outside world we all appear differently from how we see ourselves in our own minds and this, fundamentally, is one of the reasons why we drink. We drink to forget about ourselves and our problems.

Avoidance of Life

John came to see me a few years ago when at the time he was the CEO of an insurance company. He had worked his way up to this level during his 20 years with the same firm. John explained that he was worried that he wasn't good at his job. I asked him why he thought that and he replied, "I am very embarrassed to say this but I don't work hard, in fact I don't work hard at all. I earn £175,000 a year plus bonus and I can honestly say I don't deserve this income. In fact, I don't deserve this job. I feel like I am faking it. I feel at any moment I'm going to be found out and they are going to sack me. It's almost like I want to sabotage myself all the time. I tell my assistant that I am out for a business lunch but I go out for hours, buy a newspaper and drink a couple of pints in a pub where no-one can find me. It's terrible but I can't help myself."

John's high level of anxiety was of great concern and it was as clear as day to me that he had a powerful Inner Critic. John's Inner Critic was his strongest voice. And it criticised and berated him in two different ways. The first way it did this was to nag him incessantly at work, telling him that he was inadequate for his position as CEO which in reality was far from the truth. The second way the Inner Critic operated in John's life was to criticise him when he took needed time out for a lunch break because he was anxious and emotionally exhausted. This is when his Inner Critic stepped in yet again and drove him to drink. In other words, John's Inner Critic made him feel overridden with guilt for taking time out to rest and enjoy a pint, and as a result he tried to silence this nagging voice through over-drinking. John's Inner Critic held a tight grip on him and because of this, every time he tried to move out of his Inner Critic voice it consolidated its powerful position even more.

By the time John came to see me, his memory bank was stored with failure. Every way he looked at his life John felt he had failed and was a fake. His Inner Critic nagged him incessantly, telling him: "You aren't educated enough to be in this work." "Everybody else is cleverer, better and more appropriate to be CEO than you." "Who do you think you are, earning all this money? It's ridiculous."

Then he felt he had failed when he took 'time out' from work and it turned into running away and over-drinking. John rarely questioned his Inner Critic: instead, he listened to it and believed what it said to be true. In other words, he bought into his Inner Critic's propaganda. John was being suffocated and prevented from enjoying his success through not being aware of his own Inner Dialogue. Every extra pint of beer he consumed was a way of drowning out the sound of his Radio Crazy.

The Inner Critic's Development

The Inner Critic part's personality trait is to judge and criticise you. However, it is also the part that was actually created to protect you and keep you safe. And yet, through a lifetime of different experiences, the Inner Critic has trained itself to work against you not for you, and this is why it undermines your self-confidence and ability. For the Inner Critic thinks if it can get in first and gets you to listen to what it says then it will prepare you for the worst scenario, just in case that happens.

We all have an Inner Critic, but how we interpret its conversations within our self depends on the strength of our other inner voices/parts. It would be safe for me to say that during my many years of being a therapist, I have heard pretty much every Inner Critic comment made from people from all walks of life.

John's relationship with himself was managed by the Inner Critic and it held him to emotional ransom. The truth is, John is good at his work. Nobody can get away with being bad at their work for 20 years without being found out on some level. The fact is that John's Inner Critic was so powerful that it did two things: it caused him to run away and drink to avoid the anxiety of work, while at the same time he actually worked twice as hard to prove he was good at his job. This was why he was a well respected CEO. John's Inner Critic had developed in childhood and it held its position of power in his adult life through fear. The Inner Critic feared that if John's Healthy Confident Part came forward it would lose its stranglehold.

Through our sessions and by listening to the CD, John gradually learned how to release his powerful negative Inner Critic voice and bring forward the voice which had wanted to be heard since childhood; the voice of his Healthy Confident Part. Much to John's surprise and relief, he found that his co-workers responded positively as he became happier and more relaxed. And as this happened John's confidence grew, his anxiety levels dropped and his habit of running away at lunchtime or in the afternoon to consume a few pints was no longer a part of his life.

Silent but Violent

When you purchased The Drink Less Mind you did so because something stirred within you. Perhaps it is a concern about how much you drink or how much someone you care about drinks?

Believe me that not one person really knows what anybody else is thinking at any given time, otherwise we would all be mind readers.

However, what we do know for a fact is that how we talk to our self affects our outlook on life and our health. The voice of the Inner Critic is silent to the outside world, but internally its talk can be very violent and this can hold us back from achieving what we want out of life.

The point I am making is that how we talk to ourselves is a learned behaviour pattern. It is a habit, a habit that, thankfully, we can change.

Below are some of the anxiety producing knowledge which the Inner Critic loves to impose just to destabilise us on an important occasion.

The Inner Critic Rules

- It knows everything about you, from your sexual thoughts to the cellulite on your thighs, and it will remind you of this just as you are about to make love.

- It remembers even the most old and out of date information such as when, aged 10, you stole a pen from a department store and it will remind you of this out of date data just when you are about to go for that all-important interview as the Sales Director of a department store.

- It knows every time you have felt vulnerable, such as when you have been unsuccessful at cutting down on alcohol. And it just loves to remind you of this over and over again until in desperation you drink to silence it. And of course it starts nagging again the next morning, letting you know you failed once more.

- It reads other people's minds for you. It's like your own personal psychic telling you what they think of you, and a way to turn down this anxiety is to have a drink.

- It will hound you day in and day out until you give in to its demands because it is frightened that if you don't listen to it, it will have failed in its job and so, of course, you listen.

- It thinks that everybody else deals with their life much better than you do, and it will constantly compare you to anybody and everybody in any situation where you feel slightly vulnerable, making you feel extremely vulnerable, and then a drink is the only way to suppress these anxious thoughts.

- It is the part that loves procrastination and indecisiveness and prevents you from succeeding, because it has already played out the negative scene telling you that you will fail yet again. Then it will say: "Go on, have another drink to forget your problems for a few more moments."

When you feel unsafe and feel the stir of anxiety, the Inner Critic will appear in full force for it loves vulnerability. The Inner Critic thinks and believes that if it can get in first as a protective mechanism then it is doing its work by preparing you for the worst case scenario. If you do listen to the Inner Critic, then it's guaranteed you will be hesitant with your decision making. This lack of ability to make decisions leads to self-doubt and often leaves the individual emotionally frozen, unable to pursue whatever it is they truly want to do. Feeling frozen emotionally leads to the false perception that the best way to deal with this feeling of anxiety is, once again, to have a drink.

Typical Inner Critic comments from the morning after the night before:

- Do you realise that your work is on the line because of what you said last night?
- You drank him/her beautiful and then decided to bring him/her home and you can't even remember his name.
- Nice girls don't drink too much.
- Now you're going to drink and eat all day.
- You'll never lose weight because you drink and eat too much.
- Why can't you just stop at one drink?
- Your friends think you are an idiot and you are!
- Look how much money you spend on alcohol.
- You have no self-control.
- What's wrong with you?
- Be careful: you might get found out.

Alcohol and the Inner Critic

As I have mentioned before, the Inner Critic is an expert at playing on your vulnerability. We all experience vulnerable moments as we deal with life and the people and situations we find ourselves in; however, how we interpret and deal with our feelings of vulnerability depends on the life skills with which we have been educated.

One of the easiest ways to suppress the Inner Critic's voice is to drink alcohol and this is why most people over-drink. They drink to suppress the negative self talk of the Inner Critic. The aim of

The Drink Less Mind is to assist you to train your mind to deal with your Inner Critic without having to over-drink. Through doing this, you can enjoy a drink without the emotional consequences the next day of anxiety, guilt and fear.

Rating Your Inner Critic

To be rated by: Rarely (1); About Average (3); Frequently (5) – add up your scores at the end and then see the key over the page for your personal Inner Critic score.

Questions:

Rating

	1	3	5

1. I wake in the night worried about what I did yesterday.
2. I panic about what I might have said or should have said after a few drinks.
3. I feel everybody else is better than me.
4. When I'm in company I worry what they are thinking of me.
5. I procrastinate on a regular basis.
6. I am always putting myself down.
7. I feel better socially after I have had a few drinks.
8. I drink to suppress my Inner Critic.
9. I wish I had more self-control when it comes to drinking.
10. When I look in the mirror, I don't like what I see.
11. I worry that people find me boring without a drink.
12. I feel boring unless I have had a few drinks.
13. If people really knew me they wouldn't like me.
14. I feel vulnerable around people who choose not to drink.
15. I get angry when I can't say no to having a drink.
16. I question my decisions after they have been made and worry whether I have done the right thing.
17. When I say 'No' I feel guilty.
18. When I take a questionnaire like this, I'm sure that everyone else will do better than me.
19. I avoid taking risks if I can help it.
20. When I think about all the things I should have done, I feel I have wasted my life.

Rating the Inner Critic

Key to the strength of your Inner Critic:

25-44 – Weak. Congratulations, your Inner Critic is well in check. Your self esteem is high. If you do drink you don't feel guilty and you wake up feeling good about yourself.

44-74 – Medium. Your Inner Critic is strong in certain areas of your life. It could be that in your personal world you don't drink that much but perhaps professionally you do drink more than you would truly like to, or vice versa.

75 plus – Strong. Your Inner Critic plays havoc with your emotional well-being and often causes overpowering guilt and unnecessary bouts of low self-worth. You need to check in with your Healthy Confident Part more often, and know that you are making an effort to improve your relationship with yourself irrespective of what happened yesterday or what may happen tomorrow.

Your Healthy Confident Part That Likes to Deal with Life Sober

The Inner Critic is there solely to criticise you and it always will. The question is, how to deal with it.

The Healthy Confident Part represents the part that decided to read this book and it is the part that needs to be educated because it is your strongest voice, rather than your Inner Critic.

Your Healthy Confident Part is the inner voice that a 100 per cent really wants you to drink less and live more. Your Healthy Confident Part has the resources to show you and to guide you on how to look after yourself.

Your Healthy Confident Part represents the desire to drink less and deal with life sober. It is the part that knows how to truly look after you by assisting you in eating well and drinking less and, in order for it to be more present in your life, you need to educate it to feel safe. How does one do that? By using the deeper part of your mind where all your emotional software habits are stored.

The Goal of Your Healthy Confident Part

Over the next few chapters, you will be introduced to some new concepts; these will help you to gain an understanding of the different personality traits that we all have.

In order for you to feel confident to drink less, you need to bring in your Healthy Confident Part as your strongest voice. Of all the parts within you, it is your Healthy Confident Part which will allow you to deal with life with increased self-belief and self-respect, irrespective of your past. You cannot change your past but you can change your present and your future. The best way of achieving this is by listening to the enclosed CD. It is an integral and invaluable part of this book and programme. You need to educate your Healthy Confident Part to be present in your daily life. Once it is more present, you won't need to drink to suppress the Inner Critic, but rather enjoy a drink with family and friends because you want to, instead of have to.

When you have a strong Healthy Confident Part, it means that you can make healthier decisions, procrastinate less and live a happier life because you're not suppressing the Inner Critic with alcohol. This in itself is a powerful and rewarding experience because you will be managing and balancing your Healthy Confident Part.

After you have read chapter 3, you will be ready to listen to track 1 of the CD. Your mind will start to create for itself the library of how to deal with life confidently without constantly over-consuming alcohol as part of the equation. Your mind will learn through listening to the CD, and drinking less will become more comfortable; this will enable you to improve the quality of your thoughts and feelings and cope with life's anxieties.

Life is Very Rarely Perfect

Here is a little tip from me to you to help as you are reading this book and listening to the enclosed CD. As I mentioned before, the Inner Critic loves to see you fail and it loves to think it can read other people's minds. So here is a kind word from your Healthy Confident Part: "Don't try to run before you walk." In other words, do not put yourself under pressure: remember, it is all about baby steps. The Inner Critic is one smart voice and it now knows that you know of its existence and because of this it may increase its voice temporarily: because it feels threatened it will tell you: "You will fail." You will not fail, because you are already in the process of building your Healthy Confident Part as you read these words. And so your Healthy Confident Part will continue to grow stronger, while the voice of your Inner Critic will decrease in strength as it relaxes its hold.

This process does take practice, but stick with it because each day it will become easier and in a short space of time it will become an automatic part of your life. As my clients tell me: "It is well worth it." And remember, you are worth it too!

Something to Think About

Anne and John live very different lifestyles; however, they both learned to adjust the volume of their Inner Dialogue. They turned down their negative voices/parts by tuning in and increasing the volume of their Healthy Confident Part – as a result they now both live happier, more communicative and relaxed lives. They also expressed to me, individually, how thrilled they are to be out of the Radio Crazy syndrome and in control of when and how they drink. Their anxiety levels have decreased and this enables them to evaluate and identify what feels right for them.

"MY HEALTHY CONFIDENT SELF
IS SO ANNOYINGLY SMUG I HAD
TO COME IN HERE FOR A STIFF DRINK"

Chapter 3

The Software of Your Mind

Your Mind Thinks Drinking is Normal

The mind is a powerful tool and most of us in our everyday life will not need to understand its mechanics; however, the purpose of this book is to offer you an insight into the mechanical and habitual drinking patterns that are holding you back from true health and well-being. The mind could be likened to a computer that stores every memory in the emotional software that continues to produce the same habits/results unless you tell it otherwise. If you would like to change certain behaviours then you must change your software messages.

In this chapter, you will learn how to be the computer wizard of your own mind, for you have the power to change life long habits that hold you back and prevent you from feeling better about yourself: this includes your drinking patterns. You will gain an understanding of how your mind has trained itself to deal with life through alcohol, and understand how it created 'archive files' that enable it to recall life experiences from its emotional software. These files equate stress as well as social anxiety with drinking and these are just a couple that are stored by your mind. You will likely have your own personal trigger.

Using Hypnosis in Your Daily Life

You may not have previously realised that hypnosis is a completely natural state that we all enter into many times each day. It is so natural that we accept it without realising we are actually doing it. A lot of men and women I meet and work with say: "I couldn't possibly be hypnotised." However, every one of us is able to be hypnotised, either by ourselves or, if we choose, by someone else. The hypnotic state is experienced every time we daydream and I am sure we can all identify with that. A prime example of this is when we are on a train and we arrive at our destination without noticing the last five stops, or when we move into the daily automatic process of driving to work and arrive without being consciously aware of every moment of the drive. It is a state where our conscious mind starts to move into the background, as the unconscious mind starts to come forward. When you drift into sleep you must pass through the hypnotic daydream state. You cannot go to sleep without this process.

As we fall asleep our breathing starts to slow down, our heart rate drops and our circulation as well as our metabolic rate slows down. This process can take approximately 5 to 20 minutes. During this stage we are in hypnosis, and it is at this time that we become highly receptive to new learning. This is therefore a very creative time: a time when a lot of new ideas, businesses and inventions are created. And it is absolutely the right time to create new behaviours, starting with your thinking.

The Unconscious Mind

The unconscious mind is an amazingly powerful tool which can work with you and against you. We use it every second of the day and night without being aware most of the time that this is happening. There are some important facts contained in this chapter which will help you to understand why you have created certain habits and behaviours, so that you attain an awareness of the tools you possess which enable you to change the negative behaviour and enhance positive behaviour. The Healthy Confident Part is your positive part which chooses not to drink, or to drink LESS.

I always explain at the beginning of all of my workshops and seminars how the unconscious mind works, to alleviate any misconceptions participants may have about hypnosis, and now I would like to demonstrate to you the role of your unconscious mind.

Time

The unconscious mind has no concept of time. That is why, when you sleep at night, you are not aware of how long you have slept until you check your watch or bedside clock. If you were consciously aware all the time you slept, you would be exhausted. The reason why you sleep is to rest the body and the conscious mind. The unconscious mind never stops working. It is available 24 hours a day and it is fully functioning even while you are sleeping.

Your Body

The unconscious mind manages all of your bodily functions from your heart beating through to your breathing, the process of your digestion and the elimination of food and alcohol. All of this happens 24 hours a day, without you even thinking about it. How much your unconscious mind manages is almost incomprehensible. You just trust that this part of the mind knows what to do and you just let it get on with it.

Your Memory Bank

Every single moment of your life is stored in the unconscious part of your mind, and this part of the mind does not operate chronologically. If you wanted to recall anything from 10 years ago, your mind would not go back through every day, hour, minute or second until it arrived at that particular moment in time. If this was the case, you would be spending a very long time sorting through your memory bank and be unable to focus and live in the present. However, your remarkable mind is able to pinpoint a moment in time that you want to recall both accurately and efficiently. For example, if you and a friend got very drunk at the age of 13 drinking your father's special whisky and you ended up being incredibly ill then, whenever you think about whisky now you could instantly feel physically sick. This experience could have taken place 20 years ago or yesterday. The point is, your mind has the ability to locate any experience which is stored pretty much immediately and the more powerful the experience, the stronger your reaction is.

Everything is Real

The unconscious mind comprehends every experience as a real experience. Unlike the conscious mind where there is rationale and logic, this deeper part of your mind doesn't know the difference between imagination and reality. This is the most important point to remember when it comes to making positive changes, as it is the core part of the success of hypnosis.

When you daydream, your conscious vision fades and your unconscious mind's vision of whatever you are imagining becomes real. You can see, feel and hear every nuance of what that thought is about, even though, in reality, it is not really in front of you at all. When you stop daydreaming, your conscious mind acknowledges that you were daydreaming but your unconscious mind saw that experience as real.

All of our Senses are Positive and Negative

The unconscious mind works solely on emotions and memories. It uses one or more or all of the senses to recall any memories, whether good or bad. We immediately associate situations and places not just by our visual recall but by all of the senses. Personally, whenever I smell beer it immediately brings me back to my childhood and the happy times I spent with my grandfather, whom I adored. He would sit in the sun relaxing while enjoying a glass of beer. I loved spending as much time as possible with him and, to this day, beer to me signifies a 'happy liquid'.

The opposite could also hold true when the smell of beer in a glass or on someone's breath is associated with a cruel grandfather who drank too much. Then, the smell and/or taste of beer recalls childhood memories of rules, restrictions, feeling unwanted or even abused. For some men and women, walking past a pub could be an emotionally disturbing experience because the smell of beer stirs up unpleasant emotional memories. These people could refuse to drink beer because of the memory association. When this happens, it is the mind recalling instantly its most prominent example of how to deal with beer.

One Trial Learning

In hypnosis therapy, some emotional habits can be described as 'one trial learning'. This expression is used for clients who have trained their unconscious mind through one powerful and emotionally charged experience. This powerful experience then leads to a behaviour which becomes a habit.

Joseph's One Trial Learning

Joseph had a memory of his father coming home one day from work extremely stressed and upset, which was out of character for his father. Joseph loved his father and looked forward to his coming home at the end of the day. This time, however, he witnessed his normally calm father march through the front door and slam it shut. Because Joseph was unsure of what to do or how to behave, he hid while his father poured himself a whisky. As an adult, Joseph recalled peeping through the glass door and watching as his father slowly but surely with each sip began to relax and unfold into the father he loved. An hour later Joseph's calm, loving and kind father reappeared. This is a classic example of one trial learning. When we see someone who is close to us become distressed and upset and we stand helplessly by wanting to help but do not know what to do, we then file this experience away in our stored memory. Joseph's memory did just that: it filed this incident away and then created a habit so that when he was distressed and upset, whisky served as the immediate remedy for his de-stressing.

Joseph is a great example of how we are influenced by our parents' behaviour, which can affect our lives positively or negatively. The good news is that you can look back on these memories as an adult and know you have the resources within you to change.

Often, the first thing we think of when we see someone experiencing high levels of anxiety or stress is to hand them a drink to calm them down, for we, and they, regard this as an immediate emotional fix. When a person who is stressed develops the habit of downing four or five whiskies on a regular basis, they risk the fact that they are not dealing with their stress: they are, in fact, running away from it. This is when it is wise to check in with your Healthy Confident Part so that every stressful moment doesn't necessarily register in your mind as four or five whiskies on a regular basis.

Sally's One Trial Learning

When Sally was 15 she witnessed her father leave her mother in a volatile situation. Then Sally watched as her mother used alcohol as a way to cope in reaction to the pain and rejection she was going through. Sally's mother wasn't an alcoholic; however, she did frequently consume a number of glasses of wine to forget the pain. When Sally was in her early twenties her first serious boyfriend broke up with her without any explanation and she was devastated. Sally's mind scanned her memory bank to find out how to deal with this rejection – how to find a coping strategy. Without any conscious interaction, her mind remembered that the way her mother dealt with her heartbreak was through several glasses of wine and so Sally started to drink to suppress her rejection. It was an immediate, unconscious and, at the time, very effective way of reducing her emotional pain. Sally's drinking then went on to become a habit and it was having a negative effect on her life, her work and future relationships. Sally, like all people in this situation, had become a willing co-dependent on alcohol to numb the painful experience, rather than move forward from it.

The Unconscious Mind and Vulnerability

Sally is a classic example of how the unconscious mind works so efficiently when it comes to finding an immediate and 'effective' emotional support and 'eraser'. It used her memory bank or software and pulled forward its file which recalled her mother's reaction, and it did this by accessing and using all of the senses. When the emotional experience is high, the mind will find the most powerful example of how to deal with the situation even if it is detrimental to you. It is impersonal. It doesn't know the difference between positive and negative, it just knows what you have experienced and what you are now experiencing.

The conscious mind experiences the fight or flight response: 'should I stay' or 'should I run'. As a result, the unconscious mind has to make a decision as to how to alleviate the feelings of vulnerability. The unconscious mind has to find a coping strategy to deal with the adrenaline rush created.

Sally's scenario could have been different. Sally's mother could have stopped eating due to the pain and anxiety, or over-eaten (comfort eating – see The Weight Less Mind™ book). Alternatively, her mother could have dealt with the breakup in a completely healthy way too, but she did not know how and so she coped as best she could. However, the way in which she coped with the breakdown of her marriage was filed away in Sally's unconscious memories and was pulled forward when her own partner walked out with no explanation.

Working with Sally, it didn't take long before I could see she was now dealing with the pain of her breakup in a positive and healthier way. Instead of drinking to dull the pain and make it temporarily disappear, she faced her situation sober, and in the process found renewed strength as she realised that her Healthy Confident Part was an integral part of her being. Sally also recognised that her relationship had been far from perfect and that her boyfriend's walking out had been a blessing in disguise.

The Four Different Brain Waves

There are four different brain wave activities that we experience throughout every day and night.

Beta

The Beta state is called the waking state, where the conscious mind is going about its daily life involving rational thinking. It is a logical state. Therefore, it begins to plan our every day movements from eating breakfast through to buying a train ticket when we arrive at the station. The mind is rapidly working to achieve what we need to achieve in our daily life. The conscious mind is the most prominent part of the mind during this time.

Alpha

The Alpha state is the half awake/half asleep state. It is when you daydream, or when you can't remember reading for the past 10 minutes. It is a time when your conscious mind is sending the information to the unconscious mind to be absorbed, stored and ready to be recalled at any time.

During this time, the unconscious mind is very intuitive. It can be a time when you find answers to questions, resolve problems and find solutions. This is why many wellness gurus advocate quiet daily meditation.

We all need to daydream just as children do. Children between the ages of 7 and 14 are predominately in the alpha state. This is the last stage of learning to become more adult, to make logical choices and develop a sense of self.

This is the hypnotic state. It is more awake than asleep, either as you drift into sleep or at the last stage of coming out of the sleep state.

Theta

Theta is an experience of a much deeper state. Some would describe it as a meditative state, where you are highly open to new ideas. It is an experience where you may feel you have fallen asleep. It is the last stage just before you drift into sleep or the first level of awakening in the morning.

From infancy to around 7 years of age, a child will be predominately experiencing this unconscious state. Think about how much an infant has to learn in its first 7 years on this earth. It has to learn to walk, talk and make sense of the world it lives in. All of a child's senses are used to play, laugh and learn. Imagine as an adult how much fun it is to be able to enter this state on a regular basis. You can enter this state whenever you like through listening to The Drink Less Mind CD.

Delta

Delta is when your conscious mind sleeps. This is when it rests so you awaken feeling refreshed in the morning. This is also the state you are in when you are under a general anaesthetic. However, your unconscious mind is still working, making sure your body functions.

"WHENEVER I HAVE A BRAINWAVE IT'S USUALLY THAT WE SHOULD ALL GO TO THE PUB"

The Software

After having absorbed the scientific side of how the mind works, let's begin to bring it together with the Inner Dialogue theory.

As you now know, we go into hypnosis naturally many times during the day. And now, by listening to the CD, you can utilise important time out to listen to the supportive messages which your mind will then view as real and therefore, true. Your memory bank will start to file the software in your unconscious mind of who you are at this present time, rather than using the old and out of date information of how you used to drink.

Out of Date Information

Let's look at Sally again as an example of how out of date information can interfere with the desire to improve a state of mind. Sally is invited to a party where she knows her ex-boyfriend is going to be. Her Inner Critic says, "You'll need a few drinks to cope with seeing him again. What if he brings his new girlfriend?" Just add a couple of stored similar statements and Sally's mind thinks this is how to react to being exposed to the person who rejected her. Her unconscious mind believes this to be normal, but her conscious mind does not understand. Therefore it becomes totally frustrated with her, and then the vicious cycle repeats itself and the Radio Crazy begins over again. "You got pissed last night in front of your ex. You have no self control. He thinks you are a loser and you are. He'll never want you back now."

Updating the Emotional Software

If you resonate with Sally's experience or something similar, the really positive news is that your emotional software is simply out of date! Fortunately, you have the ability to shift these outdated experiences and replace them with information that reflects what you want to feel now and in the future. As the unconscious mind does not know the difference between reality and imagination, every time you listen to the CD with this book you will be affirming your Healthy Confident Part and it will build in strength so that you don't have to fall into the habitual heavy drinking cycle. So, if that truly is your goal and desire, absolutely make time for the daily listening. If you are sceptical, give yourself three weeks to see a difference. In your mind you will be storing the fact that it is emotionally safe for you to have your Healthy Confident Part as your strongest voice, so that you can de-stress without over-drinking or drinking at all. You will be in control.

As Sally listened to the CD she developed a choice of how to react, one that supported her conscious mind's wishes. Sally's mind trained itself that rejection, unfortunately, is an experience that we all have from time to time, but that it doesn't mean rejection equates to alcohol dependency. The new software for Sally made perfect sense. Sally moved on and her relationship with wine became healthy and emotionally safe.

Willpower

There is no such thing as willpower and so there is no such thing as a lack of willpower! If you have tried consciously without success to improve the relationship with yourself by drinking less so you can feel healthier, it simply means that your unconscious mind thinks this is your normal pattern. Your unconscious mind thinks that over-drinking is simply how to cope with life. When both parts of your mind are disagreeing, the unconscious mind will win the argument over the conscious mind because it thinks it is protecting you.

By reading this book and listening to the CD, you can educate both parts of your mind to work together rather than being opposing forces, then you won't want or need to drink as much and as often. Your mind is re-learning that alcohol is something to enjoy rather than abuse or rely on. When you experience self-control, you will feel liberated. As you feel liberated and enjoy all the associated benefits, sleeping better, greater concentration, brighter complexion and eyes, you will want to repeat the behaviour that makes you feel tip top and vibrant.

Repetition

There is one point I stipulate over and over again to my clients and this is it. The more you listen to your CD, the stronger your emotional computer software will become so that it understands that drinking less is a safe and natural experience. The repetition is extremely important, and those who listen to the CD every day or, at least, every other day will experience faster and more effective results.

The more you listen to the CD, the stronger the new Healthy Confident Part software will become, so much so that you will not question your self-esteem as it improves and gains in strength. The added bonus is that your energy levels will rise, and over time this positive way of living will become enjoyable. As your energy levels increase, your thought processes will become clearer and your relationship with others will improve too. You won't want to over-drink because your emotional software now believes that it is 'old hat' – because it is. It is an old way of thinking that you have moved on from. The CD will help you to sleep better and to de-stress, and you will begin to enjoy taking time out to look after you. I call it 'Me Time'. It is 20 minutes in your day when you are doing something positive for you.

Drink One Water One – The DOWO Policy

In the following chapter, we will be looking at the different emotional responses as to 'why' we drink when we truly know it is not helping our emotional health and well-being. You now know that you can train your mind to do anything and that includes cutting back on alcohol. One simple tip that I often suggest in hypnosis is the Drink One Water One (DOWO) policy. It is a simple technique but it does work. Each sip of alcohol when supported with water will dilute its effect on your mind and body. During the CD I will make this suggestion. This is a direct suggestion to your mind and the more your mind hears and feels this policy the more it will automatically do it.

" I'VE ADOPTED THE ONE WHISKY, FOUR
CUBES OF ICE POLICY "

The Enclosed CD

The enclosed CD has 2 tracks with a bonus relaxation track. You can start to listen to track 1 now. To do this you need to make sure that you are sitting or lying down in a place where you feel warm and safe and where you will not be interrupted. You must be stationary throughout the CD. If you need to wake at any time, you can do so by simply opening your eyes.

Before you start to listen to the CD, I would like to explain how it works. A lot of people have many misconceptions about what hypnosis feels like. Here are some common questions and answers regarding the CD and hypnosis.

Q. Will I fall asleep?

A. Some people do fall asleep. This will not change the results of the self-hypnosis. Remember, the information is still going into your mind. The unconscious mind is open to receive and store information 24 hours a day. It is not for you to disagree, it is a fact.

Q. When is the best time to listen to the CD?

A. The best time is before you go to sleep, but often some of my clients do not want their partners to know what they are listening to. If this applies to you, then perhaps listen to your CD during lunchtime in the boardroom, or in a room or office where you know you will not be disturbed. Some people love waking up and listening to the CD – they feel that it sets them up for the day.

Q. If I am interrupted when listening to the CD, does it mean it hasn't worked?

A. No, not at all. It just means that you haven't completed the CD track, so maybe try it again later.

Q. Can other people listen to the CD?

A. No, tell them to go and buy their own book! You made the effort, you spent the money, and they can too if they are serious about it! It is important for you to become healthily selfish and take time out for you.

Q. What if I fall asleep and listen to all of the tracks before completing the book?

A. Don't worry. Many people fall asleep whilst listening to the CD before completion. This is normal and will not affect your results.

Q. If my mind is busy, is it still working?

A. Yes, absolutely. It doesn't make any difference. You will, on some level, be absorbing the information. It will also help you to relax and you should look forward to this down-time recharge-time.

Q. If I move around while lying or sitting down will it bring me out of hypnosis?

A. No, just move around if you need to during the CD. A lot of people, when they are relaxed, recognise how much tension they hold in their body, so any adjustments are beneficial. If you want to cough, scratch or sneeze it will not make any difference.

A Little Tip

If your moment to de-stress is as soon as you come in the door and you pour yourself a gin and tonic, pop the CD on instead. This will start to break the habit of automatically reaching for a drink. In fact, you can pop the CD on whenever you feel down, negative or are having an anxiety attack about life. It will really help you to put things into a healthier perspective.

Something to Think About

You have the right to feel good about yourself.

You are now starting to build new software for your mind, that is supporting you rather than working against you.

Your mind understands now that by listening to track 1 of the CD you are on your way to dealing with life much more healthily and confidently without having to over-drink.

Now you can start to listen to track 1.

Chapter 4

The Emotional Spectrum of Life

There are many different life experiences that trigger a whole range of emotions within us. Some of them we are conscious of and others we are not. When we decide to take that first drink there is a thought process prior to it. Yes, of course, we do drink for enjoyment and we drink to celebrate but there are many times when we drink to forget. Alcohol is often used as a form of escapism and some of the emotions that sponsor escapism within us can cause damage physically and emotionally, and carry the risk of developing into a habit.

The Stress Response – Fight or Flight

The 'fight or flight' response to stressful situations is related to 'how' you drink. You have two choices: either you can stay and deal with the stressful situation or you can fly away with the assistance of a few drinks or more. Drinking is a great way to escape for an afternoon or an evening but the problem you are avoiding does not get resolved; in fact, waking up with a hangover only serves to make the problem even worse. The

Radio Crazy becomes so loud that you awake with the Inner Critic's voice reaching a crescendo, reminding you of how you failed to deal with the situation.

Every week (and sometimes daily), both at work and at home, you will be faced with stressful moments. Some situations may seem within your control, others may not. How you respond to a stressful moment created by a situation is your mind's way of telling you that you may need to adjust your emotional software.

How you function and deal with the ups and downs of life's waves depends on your mind's training. As I explained in chapter 3, the mind is like software containing many emotional archival files and it is these that create your positive as well as negative emotional habits.

Negative stress which is not dealt with can manifest itself into panic attacks, anxiety, short-fused anger, insomnia and excessive drinking, to name just a few. The unconscious mind is a powerful tool and it will protect you when it senses the smallest sign of your becoming vulnerable and this includes stress. This is why the 'fight or flight' response kicks in so that the scary feeling of vulnerability and perceived lack of control is relieved through alcohol.

This powerful surge of adrenaline, of fear and anxiety, triggers the statement 'I can't cope' then the one trial learning response comes in with a bang and, before you know it, there you are with a drink in your hand. This is a result of a micro-second response and so the next time a similar experience crops up in your life you feel the same conditioned response of the desire to drink.

We are now going to talk about the range of emotions that can trigger the desire to drink when you consciously know that you would rather not. The aim is that you will, with the help of the CD, re-educate your mind to create a new set of coping strategies for stress. This will be a new set of stress management tools that will reflect and endorse your real emotional health and happiness.

Boredom

John came to see me because he recognised that he was stressed and he couldn't work out why. John worked as an accountant in a large city firm; he had been there for many years and his competency within the job was good. When I asked him if he liked his work, he shrugged his shoulders and said, "What else can I do?" John's response is not unusual: in fact, it is quite common. John was not necessarily unhappy with his life, he was just plain bored.

He felt his life was humdrum and routine – going to work, going home, feeding the kids, cracking open a few too many beers and watching TV with his wife, then that was it, until the next day when the lack-lustre routine began again.

Boredom provides a classic trigger for men and women to over-drink. It happens because we actually relax and, for a short while, we forget the humdrum of our everyday life. Lack of stimulation and entertainment in itself can trigger a drinking session, because everything feels just a little bit better after a few drinks – or does it?

The cause of John's drinking was two-fold. First, he found himself in a rut and so he drank to alleviate the boredom of his life. Secondly, he drank because the more he thought about his life, the more stressed and depressed he became and drinking gave him the false buzz of feeling calm and the 'I don't care' attitude. I have observed so many people saying: "After a few drinks I really don't care about it any more." and so they forget for a short while, until the next day when what they were avoiding comes back, often with a vengeance.

Feeling Trapped

Drinking is a great way to alleviate what a person perceives as a boring life. Life presents us with exciting possibilities such as falling in love, having a couple of kids and a successful career and then we awaken one morning to discover the unpleasant feeling of 'is that all there is?'

Boredom and the sensations of anxiety happen because of fear, fear of the recognition of the reality of everyday life. It can be downright scary and claustrophobic when you realise how routine your daily life has become. The sensation of feeling trapped brings forward the Inner Dialogue of: "What am I going to do with my life? I feel trapped. I have two kids, a mortgage and I can't see any exciting moments ahead." The result of this form of negative Inner Dialogue is enough to drive many men and women to consume a bottle or two to relieve their boredom, while in actuality their boredom is a result of fear.

The reason why many people drink is because they don't know what to do about their boredom or how to create positive changes. Some people genuinely believe in their 'lot' and don't want to look beyond or reconsider or rearrange the bigger picture of their life. Change represents some emotional investment. These people are scared to take up new interests or hobbies and so they fall into the abyss of falsely accepting that this IS their lot in life, and so they use alcohol to take them away from it all.

John, with the ongoing help of his CD, began to look at his life from a different perspective, and through doing this he discovered that he was creating his own boredom. He realised he was boring. He had disengaged from being an active player in his life. He had parked the responsibility for a stimulating life onto his family. He was waiting for change to happen.

And so he began the Baby Step programme. The first step John took was to do something out of his 'house-bound' routine. He explained to his wife that he needed time out for himself, and she was relieved as a glimmer of hope was on the horizon. He began taking a walk after dinner for 10 minutes, which then became half an hour. To John's amazement, he discovered aspects of his neighbourhood which he had never noticed before. His level of fitness increased and his drinking decreased because he was gaining a more positive outlook. His wife became happier, too, because John returned from his walks refreshed and ready to discuss what was happening between them, their family and his work. Instead of shutting himself off through his nightly drinking, he opened up and began to discover the positives in life.

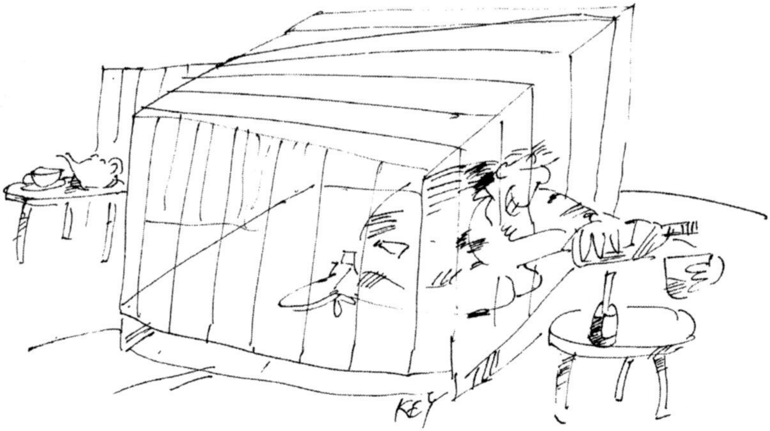
KEY

Social Anxiety

Shyness is a very common social anxiety. Many people are shy by nature and drinking for these men and women is a convenient and easy way to alleviate their shyness. Shyness comes about as we develop from the wonder of childhood into the adult world. We are not born shy. We become shy.

Many of my clients tell me that they will have a quick shot of vodka before they go to a party because they need to calm their nerves. These people are very self-conscious simply because they have developed a strong Inner Critic. The shy person's Inner Critic incessantly talks, saying: "They will think you are dumb, so you'd better have a few drinks because you're more interesting then than when you're sober." Or perhaps it will say: "You need to drink because you won't relax and enjoy yourself."

Social anxiety is, I believe, far more prevalent than we think and it is also my belief that this is one of the major catalysts which causes people to over-drink.

The Social Animal Within

When a shy person drinks, the 'Social Animal' within comes out because it feels secure at the time, and this can lead to making great friendships, relationships and business deals. Many people are naturally confident without alcohol. However, the shy man or woman may choose alcohol in an effort to hide their shyness. They use alcohol to deaden their anxiety and bring forward the familiar yet false confidence they feel they don't have.

We all admire the person who is naturally confident and adept in the art of conversation as they adapt and mingle with a group of people. The shy man or woman, however, drinks to acquire a confident persona and this can quickly develop into a habit, so when a social event occurs where there is no drinking allowed the shy person suffers panic and anxiety. This form of social occasion creates a fearful response in the shy person who needs a drink to quiet their anxiety and become confident. So they question: "Do I have a drinking problem?" My answer is: "No, you have a social anxiety disorder." They are not the same thing!

You can educate the Social Animal within you to come out without that much-needed drink. You can do this, believe me, through strengthening self-worth and confidence in yourself. There is not another person alive who can do this for you, only you. Drinking to gain confidence is a false belief, for it only serves to bring forward and accentuate your anxiety and self-worth issues. So what, you're feeling shy and a little nervous about parties and gatherings? Don't make the mistake of assuming that everyone else is fine – they may just be a little better at faking it!

Blushing

The first time Susan came to see me, she did so because she had a persistent and embarrassing blushing problem. She recalled many examples of how she had avoided certain social and work events because she was worried people would ask her questions and she would blush and fluster her words. We weren't just talking facial blushing: her neck, throat and even upper arms would colour up. Like all those who suffer from anxiety disorders, Susan had put in place many strategies to avoid these perceived potential blushing moments.   Sadly for Susan, she had rejected a fantastic work opportunity because it meant attending a lot of meetings and sober business lunches.   Her anxiety far outweighed her confidence, even though she was obviously very good at her work.   Susan's 'fight or flight' response was to fly away by not taking the position that had been offered because of her unconscious condition of blushing. Susan's family and friends did not understand why she had said no to such a great work opportunity and Susan felt trapped and angry, and her Inner Critic was having a field day.   She missed out on so much.

Susan's flight response came in the form of drinking wine to alleviate her anxiety, and the current position she held was one where drinking was part of the after work culture.   Susan admitted to me that the reason why she drank was not because she wanted to but because it relaxed her, and the knock-on effect was that she didn't blush.   In effect, it was a bodily reaction neutraliser.

In order for Susan to cut back on drinking, she needed to bring forward and educate her Healthy Confident Part to be more present in her daily life.   I made a personal CD for Susan where she learned to rehearse in her mind feeling confident and having positive discussions with work colleagues.   It was the Baby Step programme.   One small step every week, so her emotional software understood that talking while sober equated self-worth with calm confidence.   The more Susan experienced this in hypnosis, the stronger she felt to go about her daily life without drinking.   Susan still loves to drink; however, now she drinks to enjoy a glass of well-chosen wine (she has even developed an interest in fine wines) and is in control of how much she consumes, choosing to stay sober.   As her Healthy Confident Part grew, her blushing decreased until it was no longer problematic in her life.

Fear of Not Being Liked

There is so much in the media today about young people's binge drinking, which is of great concern, and it is with this in mind that I will tell you of an event I attended when I was younger. It was an eighteenth birthday party where the name of the game was for the boys to consume as much beer as their stomachs and bladders could temporarily hold. I will never forget the sight those young men presented as they actively vomited so they could drink more. Those who chose not to participate were called 'weak bastards'! Of course they weren't weak: in fact, their Healthy Confident Part gave them the courage to have a beer without joining the mêlée of drunken, vomiting young men.

There has always been and always will be a lot of pressure on youth conformity. The desire to belong, to be liked and be part of a group is important in our culture. The sad fact is that binge drinking, including underage drinking, now seems to be one of the most pressurised ways to be popular and remain popular. The one who can drink the most becomes the Queen or King Drinker for the night.

Drinking has become a sport which is proving costly, as teenagers/youths continually drink to obliterate themselves and be the best at it. There has been a rise in verbal and physical violence as well as accidents, and let's not forget the untold cost and on-going health problems which lie ahead.

I suspect there is a growing epidemic of social anxiety involved as young men and women come to terms with the stress of living in our fast-changing, transient and fickle, image-conscious world. Unsure of themselves and what is expected of them, teenagers/young adults are turning to alcohol to ease their anxiety, in the false belief that this will build their self-worth and confidence. The need to fund this habitual behaviour is another story.

I believe it is necessary for teenagers/young adults to gain self-worth and confidence through sober eyes and minds, so they gain a better understanding of who they are and what they can contribute to the world they live in. To achieve this, it is my belief that it is necessary to educate them in the behaviour of the 'why' and 'how' of drink so they may enjoy the benefits of being in control of their drinking instead of running the risk of being on the dangerous, slippery slope of alcohol dependency.

Anger

Anger is an emotion which some people can release like a puff of wind, for they blow their stack quickly and then it is over, leaving those around them with the débris. Other people do not respond outwardly in anger for they have learnt through childhood experiences to bury it, and so anger is not part of their emotional vocabulary. They keep it buried deep inside. Many men and women who feel the slightest hint of anger suppress this feeling with alcohol. They drink to drown the expression of this hot, red emotion. Those caught in the fall-out of verbal débris also often turn to a drink to make themselves feel better.

We all feel anger and ultra-hot emotions from time to time, and at times for good reason! The question is, how do you process your anger without it becoming the trigger for over-drinking? If you are suppressing your anger by drinking alcohol, then the suppressed anger becomes stored in your mind and body. Each sip is sending the anger response deeper into your software, where it is filed so this becomes your learnt and habitual response of how you deal with anger. Harbouring anger can lead to numerous health issues, and my advice is to think about how you process anger and whether it is a method that is supportive to your health and well-being or whether it is damaging it.

It may seem at the time that drinking a few beers will help alleviate your anger, but in fact it is suppressing it. You may feel better for a short period of time, but each sip of alcohol is affirming that the only way you cope with anger is to drink to suppress it. Mask it, camouflage it, ignore it. Then you wake the next morning with the anger still boiling and churning around inside you because you have not dealt with it. And so the spiral of decline takes hold. Our Inner Critic conspires to help us sabotage ourselves.

Then there are men and women who, when they over-drink, become volatile and abusive, letting their anger pour forth hurting the people around them. This is fear erupting in anger. The next day they become remorseful and riddled with guilt at the damage they have done to others, but it is often too late for their apology to be accepted. Often the offending behaviour is denied, because it is not remembered by the drinker.

Anger, when not expressed in an emotional healthy way, becomes buried or erupts like a volcano: either way, this means your mind registers that something is not right and needs to be addressed.

A person who expresses their anger in an appropriate way will use the tools of calming down to evaluate the situation, then approach the person or people involved and explain why they feel angry. This is one of the healthiest ways to deal with anger and brings excellent results.

Angry with Yourself

Many people are just plain angry with themselves. Their Inner Critic festers on things they 'should have' done or 'could have' done with their lives, or 'should be' doing to improve their lives. Their Inner Critic panics, which means they take these remarks on board as true and the only way to alleviate this fear-driven anger is to drink. This is also a very destructive drinking emotional response and is extremely painful to watch. When someone drinks in an angry response to their Inner Critic, they are doing so out of fear. This is when the Inner Critic is at its most demonic and it will hold the individual to emotional ransom, rendering them helpless and unable to reach their life potential.

There are many reasons for how we develop the pattern of our anger emotion in childhood and carry it through to adulthood. The environment in which we were raised has far-reaching effects, from having judgemental parents, parents with high expectations or angry, abusive parents; or maybe it was one of your siblings that affected your emotion of anger. Regardless of how or when we developed our anger emotional pattern, as adults we have the freedom of choice to change so we are able to drink and enjoy the benefits.

Depression

Joe phoned for an appointment as he was suffering from depression and had had enough. He had been made redundant from his managerial position in a factory after 15 years. He had two young children and a wife who was clearly stressed out about him not working for over 18 months. Money was proving tight and tensions were running high in the household.

I asked Joe whether he had been for any job interviews since his redundancy. He replied that he had been for just two interviews since leaving. As Joe talked openly to me, I sensed that there was something more deep-rooted, rather than that he just couldn't be bothered looking for work.

Joe told me that rumours had been flying for quite some time, saying the firm was planning to lay off a lot of staff, and as a manager he had found himself in the difficult position of having to let some staff go. He said he started to get anxious about his own position in the factory and had convinced himself that he would be let go, too. He started to make mistakes and turn up late, a self-sabotage system at its best. Clearly, his Inner Critic was at play here. He started thinking how other people would be better in his position as manager than he was, and when he was made redundant he drove home to his wife in tears, like a child waiting to be whipped by his parents.

Unfortunately for Joe, his wife was not that understanding and questioned him when he got home, suggesting that perhaps he did something wrong because other managers had not been made redundant. Joe's Inner Critic stepped in big time, for it was celebrating the fact that even his wife thought he was crap at his job.

The sad thing is, his wife's Inner Critic came into play too, as it told her: "What will people think – my husband doesn't have a job!" and a vicious cycle between Joe and his wife started to unfold. No wonder he hadn't been for a job interview, as he had received a double whammy: first his own Inner Critic and then his wife's Inner Critic and, to make matters worse, his parents reacted in horror at Joe losing his managerial position. This led Joe down the slippery slope of drinking to suppress the Inner Critic. Over a period of time, Joe decided there was no point in his applying for work "because I wouldn't get it anyway".

When I mentioned the Inner Dialogue theory Joe replied, "This is scary, it's like you are inside my head." I explained to him, "No, I am not in your head; however, I know what you are thinking and it is a reflection of a demonic Inner Critic which has led you to extremely low self-worth and depression." Joe's depression was situational rather than clinical and he had refused anti-depressants, for he felt there had to be another way to help him through it.

Joe and I worked on quietening his Inner Critic and strengthening his Healthy Confident Part, and as he didn't have much money our work together was restricted, so we arrived at the arrangement that I would construct a CD programme to help him. Trying to apply for jobs straight away wasn't going to work because Joe's self-esteem was just too low and so we embarked on the Baby Steps programme. He would take small steps where he did little things towards reaching his goal, such as reading through the employment section without attempting to apply for any of the advertised positions. Joe needed to start reading about what was out there and getting used to the idea of being back in the workforce. He began running again, something he used to do, and he also began taking better care of himself. As these steps increased in strength, so did Joe. He gained confidence, cut back on his drinking (which the family budget could not afford to sustain anyway), lost weight and recognised, with the help of the CD programme, that he wasn't such a bad bloke after all.

The story of Joe is a story of Inner Critic depression and we are all at risk of experiencing this, for when the Inner Critic starts to tell us we are no good and we are hopeless, we can fall into the trap of believing what it says. And so it is not uncommon for men and women who feel depressed to use alcohol in the false belief that it helps them with their depression: in fact, the opposite is true – it leads to keeping the sense of helplessness active. You need to understand how the Inner Critic works so you can win.

The enclosed CD will help alleviate emotional pain and hurt as it gives the individual time out from all of those never-ending negative thoughts. It is a time and space to relax, let go and enjoy pampering your mind. This is a wonderful gift you can give yourself as you create new, positive software in your unconscious mind.

Anxiety

Anxiety is created when there is an unbearable amount of fear and the 'fight or flight' response occurs. The unconscious mind perceives that you are once again in a circumstance that is way too stressful, and this is when a high level of anxiety or an actual panic attack takes place. The heart rate soars, sweating, fainting and being physically sick may occur. This is a frightening situation for anybody to be in and one I hear a lot of as a hypnotherapist.

Hypnosis is a brilliant tool to aid anxiety disorders. Many clients have a fear of flying and feel the need to take sedatives or drink excessive alcohol to get on that dreaded plane. What pressure it is to think that a holiday is fraught with anxiety about how you are going to get there and back, or maybe holidays abroad just don't happen for you because of your anxiety about flying. When the ordeal of anxiety is experienced, the person tries to relieve it and one of the ways is to have a drink, or two, or more and find Dutch courage.

Cameron came to see me because of his anxiety about speaking in public. He said that before speaking in public he would have the 'good luck' slug of vodka before going on stage. By the time he walked into my clinic, he was prepared to walk out of his highly paid speaking position because he was worried that he was an alcoholic. Cameron did not drink much when he wasn't speaking in public. When, after each talk, he was told how amazing his talk was, he never really believed it because he felt it was the vodka speaking not him, and so Cameron was facing a crisis of confidence and identity. I felt very sorry for him because he was obviously a great speaker but his Inner Critic had become so powerful and attacked him with statements such as: "You need the vodka, if you don't take it you might screw up and have a panic attack!" And so he became convinced that he couldn't speak without vodka.

I asked Cameron when was the first time he had drunk vodka before speaking? He replied that it started when he was at university and he was asked to make a speech which he fluffed completely, due to anxiety. He swore that never again would he speak in public, and then, low and behold, in his job he was asked to talk at a meeting which he knew would lift his professional profile. It was then he remembered that when he was studying, some students took vodka to calm their exam nerves, so with complete guilt but desperation Cameron took that shot of vodka and his talk went brilliantly.

It wasn't that he drank a lot, he did just have that one swig of vodka and yes, it did take the edge off his anxiety, but it also took his confidence away and charged up his mind with Inner Critic comments.

In order for Cameron to gain confidence, we needed to educate his unconscious mind so that the Healthy Confident Part was stronger than his Inner Critic and any anxiety it created.

Your Mind Chooses Anxiety or Relaxation

In order for you to create anxiety or relaxation, your mind needs to produce very different chemical and physical reactions. Your unconscious mind, when it recognises anxiety, sends the signal to increase your heart rate, sweating, shaking etc. To create calmness and confidence, your unconscious mind signals your body to produce lovely, positive chemicals full of happiness, health and well-being. This is a learnt behaviour.

As they say, one man's stress is another man's excitement. Your unconscious mind has to choose negative or positive. Through the use of hypnosis, you can train the mind to choose relaxation over anxiety. Developing this takes practice and patience; however, the CD in the back of this book will assist you by helping you train your mind to be calm and confident in all aspects of your life.

Procrastination

Of all of the emotional responses on the spectrum of life, procrastination probably causes the most self-doubt and anxiety deep within us. Men and women come to see me because they are not sure what they want to do in life. These people are uncertain and so they procrastinate as to whether they should change work, a relationship or housing. They sit on the fence and swing between this idea and that idea. There is a strong Inner Critic behind this sitting on the fence syndrome and in order for someone to get off the fence, they need to make a decision about what they truly want.

Procrastinators generally love drinking, because it helps them ponder what they 'should' and 'shouldn't' do without doing anything but sit on the fence. 'I'll think about it tomorrow' or 'I'll do it when this happens' are common procrastinator statements. Procrastination is also common with people who want to lose weight. They put off truly living in their life until they have lost weight and, of course, often they don't lose weight so they never get on with reaching their life's potential. You can read about procrastinators in The Weight Less Mind, my book which deals with issues related to food. Putting off positive and important life changes due to fear or self-doubt only increases a procrastinator's drinking, as they keep telling themselves they will do it tomorrow. This, of course, is due to the Inner Critic and its tirade of negativity, making the person feel inadequate and therefore unsure and unsafe at decision making. And so the procrastinator continues sitting on the fence and drinking to dull their indecision, as their conscious mind wants them to move forward but their unconscious mind holds them back.

The Emotional Drinking Chart

The following landscape chart is an example of a day in the life of one of my client's drinking habits. For your own use you can download this chart from my website: www.georgiafoster.com.

This chart is a great conscious mind tool to see where you may be habitually drinking and why. It will help you to recognise the patterns of how you drink when you truly don't want to. Use this chart for 30 days: by doing this you will gain great insight into the patterns, the people and the range of emotions that flow through your mind on a daily basis. You will recognise how your unconscious mind can trigger the desire to drink without you being conscious of it.

Read through the emotions carefully and see which ones resonate with you and each drinking experience:

- Anger
- Boredom
- Fear
- Anxiety
- Frustration

- Hurt
- Rejection
- Loneliness
- Happiness
- Love

You may also use this chart to look kindly at the people around you who may trigger over-drinking in you.

A note of warning: heavy drinkers will not like it when you decide to cut back on alcohol because it will trigger their Inner Critic comments about their own drinking issues. Do not succumb to their anxiety about you drinking less, and do not be bullied into drinking to keep them happy. It may change the relationship dynamics; however, this book is about looking after you emotionally and physically and if other people don't like it – tough! They'll just have to adjust to the new you, and they will.

Something to Think About

Alcohol contains a high level of sugar, so when you reduce your drinking you are reducing your sugar intake, therefore you may experience the craving for sugar and find yourself over-consuming sweets and chocolates or being drawn back to alcohol, not because of the alcohol itself but because your body thinks alcohol is the best source of sugar.

The dramatic fluctuations of emotions that alcohol triggers, from anxiety to depression, may lead to the desire to feel better and that means consuming sugar in any form. Gillian's advice is to look at balancing your sugar levels by having a low GI diet and taking Sucroguard (visit www.georgiafoster.com) to support your desire to drink less and consume less sugar.

Date and Time	Where were you?	Who was with you?	What triggered the decision to drink?	What thoughts and emotions came to your mind before you decided to drink?	How much did you drink?
10th February 3.05pm	Work	My boss	My appraisal review	I was nervous about discussing my appraisal. My boss is a pretty direct person. He is much more approachable after a few drinks. It was his suggestion anyway.	3 glasses of wine
10th February 5pm	After work	My work mate	Discussing the meeting with my boss	Feeling pissed off at having to feel like a child by having an appraisal.	3 pints of beer
10th February 7pm	Home	My wife	Discussing the meeting with my boss	Relieved to be home, the day is over and I can now relax. I am tired.	1 bottle of wine with dinner.
11th February	Home	My wife	A delicious meal	A delicious meal. Feeling safe.	Gin and tonic, 1 bottle of wine with dinner.
12th February	Home	My wife	A takeaway curry	Hungry/tired. Need something to drink with the curry.	3 bottles of beer, 1 bottle of wine, 1 brandy

"TOMORROW I'M GOING TO START READING A BOOK ON PROCRASTINATION."

Chapter 5

You and Your Liver

Later on in this chapter, Gillian Hamer, nutritionist and my colleague, is going to take you on a truthful journey where you will learn about:

- the adverse effects of alcohol on the body;
- the functions of the liver;
- the steps you can take to reduce the effects of alcohol.

For now, let's take a look at the interactive dialogue between you and your liver.

Imagine for a moment what it is like for your liver every time you over-consume alcohol. The liver is a hard worker, working 24 hours a day non-stop with no payment and no days or nights off! While you sleep, there it is working away on your behalf because it is an integral part of your well-being.

All of our internal organs work non-stop day and night, and when one of them decides to take some time off due to over-work we certainly know about it, for we become sick and then we spend our money or the government's money attending a doctor or health care professional to rectify the damage that we have self-inflicted.

Astonishingly, we continue this cycle of internal self-abuse of our organs through over-indulging in drink and food to the detriment of our health. Why is it that we continually sabotage our health and well-being when we know that our behaviour is leading to self-destruction?

Our liver is a totally unique piece of machinery and was designed by some force, creator or God, whichever is your belief.

The Industrial Revolution saw engineers design and build amazing machinery which transformed society and the working world, which in turn led to our present day life where computers, high definition television and film are accepted as given facts. Think for a moment about how frustrated we become when we suffer a glitch in our computer program or we flick the switch and discover the room we enter is dark because the light has gone out. We become angry and voice our frustration at these malfunctions loud and clear because we have the ability to do this, but our liver's voice is silent – or so we think. The important news is that our liver does have its very own voice but we are not aware of it and so we don't listen to what it is telling us and, in fact, we often ignore our liver's voice until it is too late.

So, let you and me discover what our liver's voice may sound like. To do this, I am going to assist you in creating your own mind and liver Inner Body Dialogue so you may understand how to listen to your liver's voice and dialogue with it. As you read through the following scenarios, you may gradually become aware of physical sensations on the right side of your body underneath your rib cage: the chances are that you may already be experiencing the physical sensations of either heaviness, fullness or occasional pain in the liver area without actually being aware that this is indeed your liver, trying to tell you that it needs attention. There is no need for alarm, as these sensations mean that you are becoming aware of how your liver physically expresses itself; if, however, you do not experience the connection do not worry, for with practice you will become more in tune with your bodily sensations and therefore able to access them more readily.

Now, just for fun, we are going to use our imagination and create in the theatre of your mind a scene: it can be on film, television or stage – the setting is entirely your choice. Do not be concerned about getting it right: just have fun and explore while you get used to listening to the dialogue between your mind and your liver. The chances are that you will also become aware of the disconnection which has taken place through the years between your mind and liver, for we rarely listen to our physical body as our mind is so full of Radio Crazy chatter.

The following dialogues have been created to demonstrate how your mind and liver communicate. It is important to remember that we are all individuals, so your mind and liver dialogue will more than likely be different from the two scenarios that follow.

Scenario One

Setting: You have just received a phone call from a person to whom you are attracted, asking you to meet them for a drink. You are both excited and nervous about the meeting and outcome.

Mind: (Talking on phone) Great, I'll see you at 6.00pm in the bar. Bye. (Ends phone call)

Liver: (Groaning) Oh, no!

Mind: Now, I've got to appear calm, I must not show how nervous I feel.

Liver: Looks like I'll be working over time tonight.

Mind: Should I drive or take a taxi?

Liver: (Excited) Drive, drive.

Mind: I'll drive.

Liver: (Relieved) Yippee!

Mind: But then again, if I take the car I won't be able to relax.

Liver: (Frustrated) Oh no, you're not going to change your mind.

Mind: Drink or drive – what will I do?

Liver: (Pleading) Drive, please drive.

Mind: Of course I could limit myself to one drink.

Liver: Yeah, I've heard that before.

Mind: I'll need a drink to calm my nerves.

Liver: (Annoyed) Yeah, and then another, followed by another.

Mind: I won't drink too much. I mean it this time – I will only have one or two drinks.

Liver: (Anxious) You promise?

Mind: I'll take a cab. That way it won't matter, I can drink as much as I want.

Liver: Here we go again. You'll drink too much and I'll have to work overtime getting rid of all that alcohol while you sleep, just so you won't have a big hangover tomorrow morning.

Scenario Two
Setting: The after-hours work drinks get together.

Mind: Better cram a few drinks down the throat before I head home.

Liver: (Pleading) How about a night off?

Mind: Just as well I can hold my liquor.

Liver: (Indignant) Hey, just a minute. I'm the one who looks after the liquor!

Mind: I enjoyed that bottle of wine at lunch.

Liver: (Angry) I didn't.

Mind: A few drinks and then home for a bottle of wine over dinner.

Liver: (Tired) 24 hours a day, no time off.

Mind: Hope I sleep better tonight.

Liver: (Angry) Last night I decided to go on a 'Go Slow' campaign.

Mind: Maybe I should cut back on the booze.

Liver: (Disbelief) Did I hear correctly? Cut back on the booze?

Mind: Yeah, perhaps I should.

Liver: (Optimistic) Yes, yes!

Mind: Maybe next week I'll cut back.

Liver: (Exhausted) If you don't cut back, I'll go on strike.

Adverse Effects of Excess Alcohol on the Body

For most people, drinking a small amount of alcohol, especially in social situations, can be very enjoyable. But there is no doubt that large amounts are poison to the body and can lead to long term health problems, putting a massive strain on many vital organs and systems.

Although many people think of it as a stimulant, alcohol actually has a depressant effect on the brain and central nervous system. It causes difficulty with speech, balance and walking and slows down reaction times as well as impairing co-ordination – which is why, of course, it's unwise to drink and drive. Alcohol withdrawal is associated with 'morning shakes' and tremors of the arms and legs, while long-term heavy drinking can lead to anxiety and depression, epilepsy and even suicide, and may damage the brain irreparably.

Alcohol irritates the lining of the stomach, which can lead to a number of digestive problems including heartburn, nausea and stomach ulcers. Chronic pancreatitis (inflammation of the pancreas), hypoglycaemia (lowering of blood sugar levels), raised blood fat levels, and cancers of the mouth, throat, pharynx (back of the mouth), larynx (voice box), oesophagus (gullet) and rectum are more common among heavy drinkers.

Excess alcohol can cause high blood pressure, heart disease and stroke. However, conversely, some research shows that small amounts of alcohol (about two glasses of wine a day) can lower the risk of heart problems.

Overdoing the hard stuff can cause changes in the composition of blood, such as a reduction in the number of white blood cells (which lowers immune response increasing the likelihood of repeated chest infections) and the blood-clotting platelets. It may even cause the red blood cells to enlarge and so not work as efficiently.

Drinking too much has been linked with muscle pain and degeneration as well as an increased risk of osteoporosis (brittle bones) in later life.

Temporary impotence – 'brewer's droop' – and lowered sperm count (a key factor in infertility) are linked to excess alcohol intake. In women, excess drinking can result in a failure to ovulate (release eggs) and so to infertility.

The development of a foetus is likely to be affected by drinking during pregnancy. Reduced birth weight, lowered reading age of a child or more severe malformations are all big risks for heavy drinking mums-to-be.

Excess alcohol can also lead to severe nutrient deficiency, not only because too much drink destroys the appetite, but also because overdoing the booze uses up vitamins and minerals in the body.

Alcohol has a significant effect on the liver, the main detoxifying plant of the body, which bears the brunt of long-term drinking. While the liver can cope with small amounts of beer, spirits or wine, excess drinking can lead to progressive liver damage resulting in fatty liver, hepatitis and cirrhosis which may result in total liver failure and death. Nearly 5,000 people a year die from alcohol-related liver disease.

Liver Functions

As the liver is so important in dealing with any alcohol that we drink, we need to look at its functions in more detail. The liver performs many vital functions to do with metabolism.

Metabolism has two main methods of action:

1. building up – e.g. making protein from the smaller amino acids which we obtain from food;
2. breaking down – e.g. breaking down sugars to release energy.

The liver is involved in:

Carbohydrate metabolism
The liver can change sugar into a special form for storage, called glycogen. This happens when there is an excess of sugar in the blood. If the blood sugar level falls, the liver cleverly converts the glycogen back into glucose. It can also make more carbohydrates from protein and fats.

Protein metabolism
Without this function, death would occur in a few days. It breaks down protein and removes the toxic part, which is then converted into urea that we pass out of the body as urine. Liver cells also manufacture a number of important blood proteins such as fibrinogen, which is essential for the clotting of blood. It also makes many proteins which are needed to transport substances around the body.

Fat metabolism
The liver stores neutral fats and breaks down others such as the fatty acids, which are essential nutrients for a range of vital body functions. Also it makes a substance which can transport various types of fats and cholesterol to and from body cells. Liver cells also make 80 per cent of our bodies' cholesterol.

It's worthwhile noting that 'good cholesterol' found in foods like olive oil, seeds, nuts and oily fish is essential for our health. If our dietary cholesterol is reduced too much, a healthy liver will make up the difference, but this vital process can be disrupted by a number of factors, including excess alcohol.

Storage
Vitamins (A, D, E and K) and the minerals iron and copper are stored in the liver, and iron is released from there when needed elsewhere in the body.

Detoxifying drugs and hormones
The liver not only breaks down toxic substances made by the body but it also detoxifies all kinds of drugs, from antibiotics and painkillers to recreational drugs and, of course, alcohol. An excess of any of these drugs means that the liver can't work as efficiently.

Making bile salts
These salts are used in the small intestine to emulsify (break down into smaller bits) fats and cholesterol.

Steps You Can Take to Help Reduce the Effects of Alcohol

There are a number of things that you can do to help your liver and my colleague Gillian Hamer will now take you through them in eight simple steps. The more you manage to incorporate into your routine, the happier your liver will be.

Step One: Water, Water, Everywhere

I'm sure that you will have read that you should drink at least 8 glasses of water a day. As this may seem rather daunting, you may find it easier to have glasses of water dotted around the house and just take sips as you go by. Another idea is always to carry a bottle of water in your bag and have one in the car and one on your desk at work so you can take a few mouthfuls. Having a glass of water before each meal is a good way to increase your intake. You should try to drink as much water as you can before drinking alcohol. It's a really good idea to drink a glass of water for every glass of alcohol consumed. Remember Georgia's DOWO policy: drink one, water one. We both cannot emphasis this enough. This will help to dilute the effects of the alcohol and may make you feel fuller and so less likely to overdo it. If you forget this tip while you're out, then drinking as much water as you possibly can when you get home really does reduce that awful feeling of dehydration when you wake up in the morning.

Step Two: Line Your Stomach with Food

If possible, have a good meal before going out drinking. Protein foods digest more slowly, thus slowing down the rate at which alcohol is absorbed, so a steak and salad before going out is a great idea. If that isn't possible, make sure that you eat a simple snack, a smoothie or milkshake, or even a few pieces of fruit. Whilst it's not ideal, even eating some peanuts or crisps from the bar will help reduce the rate at which the alcohol is absorbed. Obviously, the best thing is to drink only when you're eating. Think of the Spanish who have small dishes of foods, called tapas, when drinking.

. great tip before you go out is to take three capsules of evening primrose oil and eat a small carton of fruit or plain yoghurt. This not only lines the stomach but also seems to help reduce the risk of a hangover. (You can also take another three evening primrose capsules when you come back.)

Step Three: Tips for When Out Drinking

Decide how much you're going to drink before you go out and try to stick to your target. To do this you need to know what an alcohol unit is and how many units there are in what you choose to drink. At the end of the chapter, there is a list of recommended safe limits of alcohol for your information.

Choose who you drink with. If you know that you drink more with certain people, try to space the number of times that you go out with them.

Look at what you drink — try to have soft drinks as well as water between drinks and switch between strong and weaker drinks, as this will reduce your alcohol unit intake.

Never have your drink topped up, as you will lose track of how many units you've drunk.

Avoid being part of a round, as this usually means that you'll drink more.

Step Four: Improve Your Diet

The healthier your diet, the better able your liver will be to cope with the onslaught of heavy drinking. Incorporating any of the following will be an advantage:

Cut right down on junk food and canned fizzy drinks, as well as sugary snacks like cakes, biscuits, sweets, chocolate and pre-packaged foods, which usually have a high sugar, salt and fat content.

Eat plenty of fresh fruit and vegetables/salads (aim for five pieces of fruit or helpings of vegetables/salad a day and include vegetable soups and fresh fruit juices).

Where possible, eat organic foods as they contain fewer additives, residues and other substances that the liver has to detoxify. There is also research to suggest that organic produce contains higher levels of vitamins and minerals.

Try to eat foods that have a low glycaemic index (GI) such as wholegrain foods, brown rice, oats, peas, beans, lentils, vegetables and most fruits. There are plenty of books that cover this topic.

Foods which are especially good for the liver:

Vegetables such as carrots, pumpkin, squash, beetroot, spinach, onions, garlic, peppers and herbs such as parsley. Also sulphur-containing foods like broccoli, cabbage, cauliflower and Brussels sprouts.

Fruits such as grapefruit, any orange-y coloured fruit such as mango, papaya, peaches, nectarines, apricots, melons, plums, any berries especially blue, black and raspberries, apples, lemon/limes. Tomatoes are a fruit and are good either raw in salads or cooked.

Seeds and nuts, peas, beans, lentils and small amounts of animal protein (30-60 grams per day) like fish or organic white meat.

Step Five: Try Juicing

Freshly squeezed (preferably organic) juices are a wonderful way to give the body a boost with a good dose of vitamins and minerals. You can have one any time, but taken on an empty stomach they're quickly absorbed and have a rapid effect, so you could try having one before going out drinking, or first thing the next morning as a pick-me-up.

My favourite is: 4 carrots
1 raw beetroot
1 apple
handful of grapes
1 cm cube of peeled root ginger

Any of the following juiced are good for the liver:
Vegetables: Carrot, spinach, celery, parsley
Fruits: Lemon, grapefruit, papaya, grape

You can buy a juicer at a reasonable price from most department stores, some supermarkets and electrical shops. Believe me, it's a great habit to get into. If you don't have time to make your own juice you might be able to buy them from a local shop.

Step Six: Some Hangover Tips for the Morning After

- Drink as much water as you possibly can.
- Hot water with ginger crushed in it helps with nausea and settles the stomach.
- A freshly squeezed juice/smoothie and/or some wholemeal toast with marmite may improve your energy levels.
- The homeopathic remedy, Nux vomica, helps with the nausea and supports the liver. Take one or two tablets when you wake up and repeat every two hours for up to six doses.
- Take the supplement Hepaguard Forte – one with breakfast and dinner (see Step 8 for more details).

Step Seven: Liver Cleanse

If you have any medical condition you should consult your doctor before doing this.

There are plenty of books available on this subject. The two detoxes that I've tried and survived (and felt great afterwards) are:

Liver Flush: easy on the body and simple to make. Do the flush for 10 days and then have three days off, then repeat, so this is a 23-day exercise. You can do it as often as you like but twice a year is good.

Make up one cup of freshly squeezed citrus juice (e.g. orange or grapefruit) with some lemon or lime and put in a glass jar with a lid.

Add 1-2 cloves of freshly crushed garlic and a small amount of ginger

end to use a garlic crusher for both but you could grate the
into a saucer and then squeeze the juice out).

blespoon of high quality olive oil, shake and drink.

Good to follow with a herb tea such as peppermint, or dandelion coffee.

Drink the flush in the morning and don't eat anything for an hour.

If you want to try a more intense liver and gallbladder flush, I suggest
you buy: The Amazing Liver and Gallbladder Cleanse by Andreas
Moritz (Namaste Publishing) and do the flush described in chapter 4.

Step Eight: Supplements

If you're a regular heavy drinker (i.e. you drink more than the
recommended units of alcohol per week) or binge drinker, I strongly
recommend you take the following Biocare supplements to help
support your liver and immune system. If you would like to purchase
any of these supplements please see Georgia's website:
www.georgiafoster.com.

Hepaguard Forte: 1 with breakfast and 1 with dinner
Potassium Ascorbate (vitamin C 500mg):
      1 with breakfast and 1 with dinner
Bio-Acidophilus: 1 with breakfast and 1 with dinner

If you have stopped drinking heavily, the following combination of
supplements should help to repair some of the damage:

S.M.A.R.T. UK Complex: 1 a day with food
Hepaguard Forte: 1 with breakfast and 1 with dinner
Bio-Acidophilus: 1 with breakfast and 1 with dinner

Take the above for three months at least.

Recommended Safe Limits of Alcohol

Men should not drink more than 21 units of alcohol a week (and no more than four units in any one day).

Women should not drink more than 14 units of alcohol per week (and no more than three units in any one day).

Pregnant women: if you have one or two drinks of alcohol (one or two units), once or twice a week, it is unlikely to harm your unborn baby. However, the exact amount that is safe is unknown. I always recommend little or no alcohol during pregnancy.

What is a Unit of Alcohol?

One unit is 10ml (1cl) by volume, or 8g by weight, of pure alcohol. For example:

One unit of alcohol is about equal to:

- Half a pint of ordinary strength beer, lager, or cider (3-4% alcohol by volume); or

- A small pub measure (25ml) of spirits (40% alcohol by volume); or
- A standard pub measure (50ml) of fortified wine such as sherry or port (20% alcohol by volume).

There are one and a half units of alcohol in:

- A small glass (125ml) ordinary strength wine (12% alcohol by volume); or
- A standard pub measure (35ml) of spirits (40% alcohol by volume).

A more accurate way of calculating units is as follows. The percentage alcohol by volume (abv) of any drink equals the number of units in one litre of that drink. For example:

Strong beer at 6% abv has 6 units in one litre. If you drink half a litre (500ml) – just under a pint – then you have had three units. So three pints of beer three times a week is at least 18 units. That is nearly the upper weekly safe limit for a man.

Wine at 12 abv has 12 units in one litre. If you drink a quarter of a litre (250ml) – two small glasses, then you have had three units. So a 750ml bottle of 12% wine will contain 9 units. If you drink two bottles of 12% wine over a week, that is 18 units which is above the upper safe limit for women.

"I'D LIKE ANOTHER MARTINI AND MY LIVER WILL HAVE ONE TOO."

Chapter 6

Sex and the Inner Child

What is the Inner Child?

Every time I work with my clients locating and connecting with their Inner Child, they experience a melting pot of emotion and feelings, and, to be honest with you, every time I work with my own Inner Child, I also experience powerful emotions. The most powerful feeling is to experience and realise your unique vulnerability. The Inner Child is pure and unadulterated vulnerability and is a major player in the Inner Dialogue approach.

The Inner Child is the part within us all that loves to play, cry, be touched and loved. It is the raw emotional state which can hold you back throughout your life because it may have been suppressed in the process of your developing into adulthood. If you had to grow up emotionally before your natural childhood age or you grew up in a family where affection was scorned or withheld, then your Inner Child will have learned very quickly that asking for love and affection will only get you into trouble. When the Inner Child becomes frightened, it hides away deep within the unconscious mind, often only making an appearance at certain times, as is demonstrated throughout this chapter.

The Inner Child is the wonderful loving part within all of us, and the great thing about exploring your relationship with your Inner Child is that it can lead you to a much deeper and more powerful knowing of who you really are. Spending time and exploring this part means you will become more whole in how you view yourself and the relationships around you.

The Inner Child part only knows how to live and be in the present moment and this can be a difficult and intense experience for many men and women, and they suppress their adult part through alcohol to free their Inner Child so they can access the freedom to joke and have fun.

The questions listed below are a reflection of the Inner Child behaviour. As you read through the questions, check in with yourself as to how and when you have experienced these emotions and feelings. Was alcohol involved for you to feel free enough to express yourself in the following way?

- When was the last time you had a real belly-laugh?
- When was the last time you had a really good cry?
- When was the last time you wanted to be stupid?
- How often do you rebel like a naughty child?
- When was the last time you enjoyed being loved?
- Do you feel safe in intimate situations?
- Do you often feel isolated from people, with a sense of loneliness?
- Do you often feel sad?
- Is anger something that you find hard to express?
- Do you find anger is overused in your life?

All of the questions above are related to the different emotions of the Inner Child who lives in each and every one of us. Therefore it is completely natural for us to experience all of these emotions at various times throughout life. In this chapter, we will look at these emotions in greater detail so you can become familiar with the power of your Inner Child and how it can use alcohol to express itself.

Childhood

The Inner Child is the child-like part of us that has never grown up, and it is the part within us that should never grow up, for its sole purpose is to keep us in touch with our unprocessed emotions.

Some people, unfortunately, have very few pleasant memories of their childhood. I do not know any man or woman who could say they had an unblemished and therefore perfect childhood. Most parents try to do their best for their offspring, yet often their ways of parenting may be about how they themselves were parented. However, even their best intentions are at times perceived by the child as not what they want or need. Most children adore their parents and make the unconscious assumption that their parents must be right. Every child interprets life differently within the family circle and it is this interpretation that is filed away in the software of the child's mind. The Inner Child of the unconscious mind desires only to receive love, warmth, safety and to have fun, just as you wanted to in childhood. If you cannot recall these desires being met by your parents or family circle then your Inner Child may have been suppressed earlier than normal.

This chapter takes a powerful look at our life through our child-like eyes. Do not be concerned if you find yourself experiencing tears, laughter, anger or embarrassment as you read (or you may experience the opposite) and you will find yourself gaining a greater understanding of you and your Inner Child and its effect on your life.

Becoming More Adult

If you had to grow up too soon – before you were ready – due to circumstances that were beyond your control, your adult part would have been created early in life to protect your Inner Child from being wounded. And so you became more adult as a way to protect your feelings of fear and vulnerability, and this was a natural protective reaction.

Your adult part is the part of you that now takes life too seriously, for it does not know how to laugh and enjoy life and has a real problem with 'you' just being in the moment. If this is the case, then as an adult you will consciously demonstrate being logical and organised, for you do not like chaos.

The Inner Child and Alcohol

The child within you, when suppressed, will have the passionate desire to come out from hiding from time to time, rather like daring to escape! The Inner Child loves both alcohol and food, as it feels these are fun ways to achieve the sensations of the warm glow of feeling safe, and calm, and loved. These feelings within you can become the trigger to over-drink, and you consciously crave to repeat those safe, warm feelings this substitute behaviour brings.

When we drink, the Inner Critic becomes suppressed and the Inner Child comes to the forefront because it wants to have fun, passion and excitement. It wants to play! And to achieve play time it may develop an 'I don't care' attitude. Many men and women need to drink so they can make love, give love or just have fun.

The Inner Child loves alcohol, because alcohol is the key to the gate of the garden and so it has the freedom to come out and play. This means it breaks free and finds itself allowed to tell a person that they are wonderful or to tell another a joke. The Inner Child can't wait for you to have a few drinks, because this means your Inner Critic will quieten down and its voice will be heard instead.

The Inner Child adores being adored and that is why it will find drinking with people who love to drink a safe harbour; it also enjoys finding new people to play with because, when sober, the adult man or woman may not be able to offer the love and warmth that the Inner Child can.

Allow yourself to imagine how much fun you could have with your Inner Child, if you gave yourself permission to be that child, without a drink!

The Inner Child Loves Sex

The Inner Child is the free-thinking, sexual and sensual part which exists within each and every one of us. The Inner Child loves being hugged, kissed and intimate. It is the part within us that has passion and creativity and enjoys having sex because it is an experience of being 'in the moment', of feeling safe and not alone.

Intimacy in a loving relationship is a wonderful experience which we all deserve to have, and how we achieve intimacy depends on our Inner Child's idea of how to get the intimacy it wants. It is a primitive part that doesn't think about the future or end result – all it wants is for its needs to be met right now.

Steven came to see me with intimacy issues. He had had many girlfriends, all of whom he had walked away from because they always wanted more commitment. He told me that having sex was fine but when these girls wanted to stay the following day and hang out with him he felt himself back off. Sex was all he wanted – any further contact was not on his agenda. He said he would rather go out with his mates because it was easier than making the effort to converse with a girl and continue the conversation the next morning. He was not comfortable with sharing more of himself.

I asked Steven if he enjoyed sober sex, to which he replied, "I have experienced sober sex but I would prefer not to. I can manage hungover sex, but when the girl wants to hang around it drives me crazy because I know at some stage we may have intimate discussions. I just wish they'd have sex and leave."

This was quite telling. Steven's Inner Child felt unsafe to be intimate without alcohol. His anxiety about a girl getting to know him sober was clearly of concern to him. No wonder he couldn't commit to a relationship, for it registered way too high on the scale of his vulnerability.

.even told me that he really did want to settle down with a girl and have a long-term relationship but he didn't think that would ever happen. He was right, for his sober adult ran away from being intimate. I explained to Steven that it would be virtually impossible for him to even think of a relationship until he dealt with his fear of intimacy, as it would be unfair and only result in pain and disappointment. Steven wanted to break free from the cycle of drinking himself numb for it had not achieved the outcome he wanted. He had acknowledged that he did not feel great with his drunken-sex behaviour. This realisation, which led him to see me, was a personal breakthrough.

We talked about the Baby Step programme and how locating his Inner Child when sober would help break his fear of intimacy. It did seem daunting to Steven at first, but he was desperate and agreed to embark on the Baby Step programme. Steven listened to the CD which I made for him, and part of the process was to imagine, while sober, the sensations of skin on skin, lips on lips and the association of warmth, safety, love and respect. Each week while listening to the CD he progressed, as his adult mind got used to the idea of just kissing a woman when sober, then enjoying taking her clothes off and, at each sober stage, feeling safe. He did not have to have sex, just to take sober baby steps one at a time. This is an important part of intimacy. All too often, men and women rush to achieve orgasm instead of taking their time to enjoy the baby steps. To be more emotionally engaged in the act of making love, rather than just performing a sexual function, directly feeds your sense of self.

Steven started to notice his shy Inner Child was gaining in confidence and he became aware of feeling more sexually aroused around women when sober. He also noticed that he was actually enjoying female company more and, in his words, "They're alright, you know. Girls don't just want to get married and settle down."

Steven is a classic example of the conflict that can rage in our minds. One part wants to be loved while the other thinks it is unsafe to be loved. In order for Steven to affirm that intimacy was a safe experience when sober, he needed to embrace his Inner Child – without over-drinking. Alcohol-free days (AFDs) were an essential part of our work together as I wanted him to know and experience what it felt like to be clearer in his mind and body.

I recently saw Steven walking down the street laughing and holding hands with a woman while smiling into her eyes, and it was 10.30 in the morning.

'Drink Beautiful' Syndrome

Sandra was single and not happy about it. After our second appointment, Sandra tearfully confided to me her real concern. "I love sex but don't have the confidence to approach men unless I have had a few drinks. I can't tell you how many times I have woken up with someone who I 'drank beautiful' the night before, only to realise that he was so not me! I get so angry and tired of this experience." Sandra's tears flowed as she continued. "There was this one guy who I truly did fancy. I didn't need to drink him beautiful – he just was. I had a few wines and then I started joking around. In hindsight I realise that probably a lot of girls would have fancied him. I went back to his house knowing full well that we would have sex. He was self-centred and extremely cocky. We had sex, slept for a few hours and then he said I had to leave. I was so shocked and hurt." Sandra's tears flowed even more as she recalled this painful memory. "He said to me: 'Listen, you're not my type. I only go for blondes.' I was so upset but I had drunk my money away and I had no mode of transport or money for a taxi, so I lay there stifling my crying while he snored. I thought how I did not want to do this again. Why did I do this to myself? If I hadn't drunk so much I wouldn't have put myself in this position!"

Sandra continued: "To make matters worse, when I was getting dressed in the morning I overheard him talking on the phone to his mate and he laughingly said, 'You could feed her a bale of hay before a plate of sandwiches!'"

Valuing Yourself Sexually While Sober

Sandra had good reason to be distraught, for in one night what little sense of self-worth she had had been annihilated. After having sex with a series of men she seemed unable to find a partner who would respect, love and commit to her. Sandra's Inner Child was desperate to be loved and to give love and this was why, after a few wines, her Inner Child kept saying: "Gosh, he's nice – you need love, come on: let's keep drinking so that we can be hugged tonight." Sandra's Inner Critic was nowhere to be found as she drank numerous glasses of wine and then went home with a man and had sex, then the next morning her Inner Critic began its condemnation of her behaviour of the night before. Sandra was in emotional turmoil and needed to understand why she kept repeating this self-defeating cycle of sex and self-disgust.

"I KNOW YOUR INNER CHILD MIGHT LOVE SOME MORE SEX BUT MY INNER CHILD IS KNACKERED AND WANTS TO GO TO SLEEP."

I asked Sandra if she had experienced sober sex. Her response was: "Yes, I have when I have been in a committed relationship." Then she stated that she had started going out with her last two boyfriends after a one night stand. In Sandra's mind, alcohol freed her to meet men and have casual sex in the false belief that this was the only way of beginning a relationship. Sandra had got herself into a rut of going out and getting drunk with the perceived idea that when sober she wasn't playful or likeable enough to have sex.

In order for Sandra to acknowledge her Inner Child sober, she needed to find an outlet where she could play and feel valued without necessarily embarking on a sexual liaison. When I asked Sandra if there was anything that she thought she would enjoy doing, she answered without hesitation, "I'd love to learn Italian." When at school she had enjoyed learning and was very good at French. I put forward the idea to Sandra that she find an Italian language course and renew her joy of learning.

Sandra began listening to the CD that I made just for her and she soon took the first step in the Baby Step programme. She enrolled on an Italian language course where she met a new group of men and women. After class they would have a drink and chat about what had happened that evening. There was one particular man named Frank who Sandra was drawn to; however, this time she followed the Drink One Water One policy (DOWO) and remained sober. Little by little, she and Frank got to know each other and much to her delight he asked her to meet him for dinner. Sandra was worried about what would happen; however, she stuck to her DOWO plan and when after dinner he asked her back to his place, she politely answered no. Frank accepted her refusal and escorted her home, where she enjoyed a long and passionate kiss. Little by little, by remaining sober, her Inner Child came out to play and Sandra discovered the joy of taking it slowly and getting to know Frank. He enjoyed the process too, for they had common interests and enjoyed laughing together. Sandra has referred many people to me since our work together and I recently heard that her relationship with Frank was going well.

Alcohol Means the Inner Child is Allowed Out to Play

Alcohol is used by a lot of men and women as a way for their Inner Child to come out to play. How many people drink to bring out their playful Inner Child? Quite a few, and this is okay; however, when it has become an emotional habit due to the fact that we mistakenly believe drink is the only way to access the Inner Child, we lose the sense of the fun person we really are. We are also at risk of losing our personal credibility and self-respect.

Thank goodness our Inner Child never goes away, and this is something we need to understand and continually work with. Our Inner Child state is the essence of who we are. Sadly, through life experiences, it can become suppressed and we feel that it has gone away and left us until we begin drinking: then, lo and behold, it releases itself and presents itself to the world. How often we see people who are quite serious by nature becoming, after a few drinks, much nicer, softer and kinder. The more we practise releasing our Inner Child whilst sober, the more we will remember the feeling and start to own it.

Taking Life Too Seriously

I know many people who scorn laughter and life frivolity when they are sober but after a few drinks begin to laugh and enjoy themselves. A client of mine once said to me, "You can tell if a person is an alright type after a few drinks because if they let their hair down and don't take themselves too seriously, I know they are okay, but if they drink and become miserable I'm not interested in them."

Many people have trained themselves emotionally through the software of their mind that drinking is a perceived laughter pill and without it, life is just plain hard.

Expressing Tears

The Inner Critic can become suppressed when we drink and we can become funnier and more out-going, and we take more risks. Our behaviour may become sillier and both men and women who don't normally cry can experience tears during this time. We may become tearful because we don't care much about the consequences until we wake the next morning and have a massive Inner Critic attack. The Inner Critic says, "You were such an idiot last night, what did you think you were doing? Everybody is going to laugh at you when you go into work on Monday. People are going to think you're screwed up because you couldn't stop crying." The list goes on and on; however, the fact is that the Inner Child felt safe to come out and cry because the Inner Critic had gone away.

Shutting Down the Inner Child

The Inner Child does not know about responsibility – it only knows how to 'be' and in the adult world some of us mistakenly believe that being responsible as an adult means shutting down the Inner Child part. It's also possible that maybe, along the way, people close to us have said things like: "You're not a child any more" or "You can't do that at your age". To these people, adult behaviour means good work ethics, social standing and not rocking the boat. Who among us really wants to be serious and responsible 24 hours a day? The answer to this question is a resounding 'no-one'!

A child who has experienced sexual, physical or emotional abuse will learn very quickly that remaining a child only exacerbates more abuse. Therefore, shutting down this innocent, wide-eyed, beautiful part of the self is the best method of protection. To these adults, being a child signals hurt, abandonment and abuse, so their Inner Child digs itself deep inside the unconscious mind. Why would you want to remain a child if this is what represents childhood memories?

In this situation alcohol could be the button of self-destruction and this could lead to alcohol dependency, drugs or worse. If you feel that this is your situation and that you are suffering as a result of childhood abuse, then seek counselling to help heal your Inner Child.

Self-Expression

Depending on your environmental upbringing, you may have experienced alcohol as either a way of celebrating good news or getting over stress, or it may have been used as an aid to help communication. If you came from a family where self-expression was difficult, then the chances are you will use alcohol in adulthood as a way to free yourself to talk emotionally.

Women in general are relatively good at self-expression and men appear to find self-expression more difficult. I believe it is because many of us have become stereotyped into the belief that men don't talk intimately, or about intimate emotional things, but women do. I do think this is true to a certain extent, not because it is a statement of fact, but more because men find it difficult to express their need for love because their Inner Child has been suppressed. Young boys, to this day, are still told: "Big boys don't cry." Of course this is a fallacy, and only serves to create men who are scared to show their feelings.

I believe we all have the right to the sober self-expression of enjoying our life. For many people it does take practice to free the Inner Child and have fun without alcohol; however, it is an incredibly rewarding experience.

Anger and the Inner Child

Anger is a big one when it comes to the suppression of the Inner Child, for anger is a major player in the expression of the hurt and wounded child. Once again, when alcohol is consumed, the angry Inner Child can come out and be spiteful, hurtful and abusive.

A wounded child can resort to alcohol, food or drugs and be attracted to abusive relationships simply because this is the only way the Inner Child knows how to be. It is sad but true: there are many wounded inner children walking around in adults, just waiting to express their anger, and this anger plays a major role in expressing the hurt and rejection these adults felt during their childhood.

If when you drink you become angry, tearful and fearful, it is because your Inner Child does not know how to get love and receive love. It never experienced love while you were growing up, so how can it possibly know now, and because of this it feels lost.

As mentioned before, not everyone has had a healthy childhood, and if you feel alcohol brings out these negative emotions please trust that the alcohol is demonstrating to you that you need to heal your Inner Child and that alcohol is not helping, rather it is bringing up all the pain that you need to deal with. There are many counsellors who are trained in Inner Child work.

In chapter 3, you will have read how each of us while growing up created emotional habits to enable us to cope and get on in life. Each of these habits developed at the time as an emotional reflex action and this happened because we have, in childhood, limited knowledge of the world around us. Remember: food, love, tears and laughter are the first learned experiences in life. No wonder so many of us use alcohol as a way to nurture and bring forth our Inner Child.

The Word 'No'

The Inner Child loves binge drinking because it loves being naughty and rebellious. It is also about being self-indulgent as it may have experienced the feeling of being sick on sweets as a child because saying 'no' was not acceptable. The Inner Child does not like the word 'no' and does not understand limitations as this is an adult trait. So, the more you drink, the more the child comes out and the Inner Critic suppresses itself.

The Inner Child within us all is open to exploring new experiences and loves new and exciting things. As we know, children get bored very easily and entertainment is high on the agenda: ask a parent and they will tell you this is so. When a child is told 'no', the immediate reaction is to rebel or withdraw because the child does not understand that 'no' means 'absolutely not'. A child does not have the capacity to comprehend all the rules and regulations of adult life and nor should it, therefore people who struggle with their drinking habit may have this rebellious streak or retreat in them, so they react against the word 'no'.

The Confident Fun Inner Child

How wonderful it is to see a child who is encouraged to embrace their childhood fully. There are three aspects of the confident child: the child that is allowed to be naughty while being safely cautioned and guided through their parents' unconditional love; the child who is encouraged to speak up and to be heard so they can express an opinion; and the child who has the freedom to play and have wildly creative thoughts. I love to hear a child's delightful laughter and see the beauty in the smile on his or her face.

If you feel this was not part of your childhood, you can embrace these experiences as an adult. It is your right to be the version of you that you want to be! It does take practice but the lovely thing is your Inner Child is easily accessible. You can create new learning for yourself through your inner parents' eyes, not the parents you had or have but your own ideas of how you would like to parent your Inner Child – through doing this you can access and bring out your own confident, fun, child-like part while feeling safe.

Here is some 'play work' that can assist you to explore your own Inner Child safely, so you can enjoy spending more valued time with you and the innocent, fun-loving person you are and deserve to be.

Imagination

As the unconscious mind doesn't know the difference between reality and imagination, find time to lie on your bed or sit in a chair, close your eyes and spend some time with your Inner Child. Do you have a clear image of yourself as a child? If not, look at a photograph or create an image in your mind that you feel best represents you as a child. Let your mind talk to him/her, comfort your Inner Child by telling it that it is now safe and you are available as the inner parent at any time to hear and answer its call for help. Tell your Inner Child that you are always there now no matter what happens, and that it is safe to be loved, to have fun and enjoy the wonders of life. I do warn you that this can be a highly emotional experience. Be prepared for some tears. It can be a very cathartic experience and a well-deserved one. You have the right to embrace your Inner Child because no-one will ever be able to know your child the way you do. It is a very special relationship, a bond that will always be there. An Inner Child when nurtured will give you so much emotional support, laughter and lightness in your life, and the best thing of all is that your Inner Child doesn't cost you anything!

Something to Think About

Nature
Take a walk on your own to a place where you know you feel safe. Perhaps walk through a park, then take the time to sit and look at the beauty of nature. When we view nature through the eyes of the inquisitive child, we notice how much beauty there really is in this world. Notice the birds and the colours of the trees. If it is summer, explore the flowers, their perfume, the grass beneath your feet and the height and colour of the trees. If it is autumn, run through the autumn leaves, then have fun exploring, scatter them with your feet, scoop them into your hands then lift them high and let them fall. If it is snowing, make a snowman, snowballs or a snow angel. To do this lie on your back, arms spread out at shoulder height and wave your arms through the snow, then stand up and look at the beauty of the earth angel you truly are. If it is spring, notice how the buds are beginning to come out, enjoy exploring each flower and tree and notice how men, women and children smile as they enjoy the first signs of spring. Explore with your senses: touch, taste, smell, sight and hearing, for this is how a child explores and learns.

The Movies
Rent a really funny movie on your own or with someone you feel you can really be yourself with. Laugh like you want to laugh rather than

suppressing it. Hire a movie that is a real tear-jerker and have a fantastic cry all on your own. Laughing and crying are great ways of releasing the tensions, fears and anxieties of the Inner Child.

Writing

Write a letter to yourself explaining that you did the best you possibly could as a child with the resources that you had at hand. Explain to her/him that now as an adult you are going to make sure that you and your Inner Child can safely express to each other any emotions of fear, rejection, abandonment and love.

Make a list of all the things you would love to do that you feel a little silly or shy about doing. An example of this could be joining an art or dancing class that you've always wanted to but felt too scared to try. Perhaps you could go to a pop concert that your adult part says you're too old to go to. Don't listen to your staid adult part – you have given yourself sober permission to go out and have fun because you are never too old to have fun and enjoy life.

"I TOLD MY WIFE I WAS LOOKING FOR MY INNER CHILD AND SHE SAID SHE WAS STILL LOOKING FOR MY OUTER ADULT"

Chapter 7

The Pleaser

What is the Pleaser?

Whenever I introduce the Pleaser to clients and workshop participants, I notice awkward smiles appear on many faces and I can identify with these awkward smiles, for the Pleaser part is one that is close to my own heart. It was, and still is, one of my strongest parts. On the positive side, I have to say 'Thanks' to my Pleaser for being my front-of-house personality, because it led me to this profession. However, the negative side of my Pleaser led me to many years of self-loathing.

You can spot a Pleaser a mile away because they are always willing to do things that often other people are not.

Questionnaire:

- Do you over-commit to keep everybody happy?
- Do you feel guilty if you say no to people?
- Do you play over in your mind what you previously said, worrying that you might have offended someone?
- Do you keep the conversation going to avoid silences?

- Do you worry about not being liked?
- Do you have a lot of acquaintances?
- Are you the social secretary for your friends?
- Do friends dump their problems on to you, knowing that you will pick up the pieces?
- If somebody does something awful to you, do you say it's OK when really you want to give them a piece of your mind?

The Pleaser and Fear of Not Being Liked

The Pleaser is the part within us that harbours the fear of not being good enough or liked enough, and this is a reflection of low self-worth. Pleasers are a lot of my client base for concerning reasons. If you are a Pleaser, you will notice that you spend a lot of time worrying about looking after other people to the detriment of your own health and well-being. Pleasers are constantly checking in with people to make sure they are OK, rather than checking in with themselves, because they don't see themselves as important enough. They constantly undervalue themselves and overvalue the people around them.

I was, at one stage, thinking about calling my self-esteem book 'I used to be a doormat' because that is how a Pleaser sees themselves, as something for people to wipe their feet on. It sounds awful; however, it is true.

The purpose of the Pleaser is to keep everybody else happy. It is the part that makes sure everyone else's needs are met first. The Pleaser's personality is often charming, open and warm to the outside world. It is a very attractive character trait to have, because you will be well liked. The down side is the more you look after someone else, the less time you have to look after you.

Pleasers are Popular People

Pleasers go out of their way to make sure everyone has a drink and that anybody who looks like they are being left out will be nurtured with attention. The result is that everybody loves the party Pleaser and if you resonate with this part you will be a popular person to have around. You will have a lot of invitations to different functions because you fill the silences at dinner parties, you encourage self-esteem in others and you will drink with them to make them feel better about themselves, even if you don't want to.

Pleasers are lovely people because they are good listeners and will always entertain the idea of co-ordinating other people's lives because they need to be useful. The shame of it is that by keeping busy pleasing others, the Pleaser has no time left energetically or emotionally for pleasing themselves.

The word 'NO'

Most people love having a Pleaser person in their lives, because they do the things the other person doesn't like doing. Pleasers say yes to everything because they are frightened that if they say no, they will be rejected. The irony of this is that, deep down, the fear of being rejected is actually more important to the Pleaser than the person they are pleasing, and this is the reason they say yes.

If they say no, their Pleaser will say, internally: "That person is offended" or "If you don't say yes, they may not ask you again and then you won't have any friends".

The word 'no' stirs too many fearful emotions in the Pleaser and these are the emotions of rejection, abandonment and being left out.

Mary came to see me because it was becoming increasingly obvious to her that drinking was 'infecting' her work. Late nights and hangovers with friends were proving too much for her physically and emotionally and this is what she said:

"I have a lot of friends and there always seems to be something going on socially. I feel like I can't say no because I might offend them. I worry about how much money I am spending as a lot of my friends earn more than me. I am so in debt and each outing incurs more debt. I feel sick about the fact that I know I need to say no more to going out but I am worried my friends might not like me. I smile to the outside world but inside I feel like such a loser, in fact I am a loser."

Mary was a classic Pleaser who was extremely stressed out, not just about hangovers and losing friends but also about getting out of this debt problem, too.

Pleasers and Money in Abundance

Pleasers are always spending money on other people because it is a way of being liked and respected. Unfortunately, they do this because they don't respect themselves and find themselves in some serious pickles, and one of them is being short of money. They pay for other people's meals and buy scrooge people drinks with the false belief that this will make the other person feel better.

The other side is that scrooge people love having Pleasers in their lives because the bill always get paid, of course, by the Pleaser.

In Mary's case this was true: she had got herself into a very difficult situation and the more she worried about her 'true' situation the more she went out with her friends so she could forget her self-loathing and disgust. In her mind, paying for other people's drinks wasn't so bad because it meant she was liked. She was damned if she stayed home and she was damned if she went out. She couldn't win with such a strong Pleaser.

Low Self-Esteem

If you have a strong Pleaser trait you will have low self-esteem and it will be reflected in overdoing things for other people so you can avoid looking at yourself, for when you do look at yourself all you see is a person who is 'useless'.

I have used the following statement in this book and often refer to it in my clinic work: 'If people really knew me they wouldn't like me.' This is a true Pleaser statement and it comes in all shapes and sizes, from homemakers and golfing pros through to lawyers. The Pleaser lives in all strata of our society.

The Pleaser will affirm this as a true statement and will hide it by being everything to everyone, and this includes drinking when you don't want to.

Be Careful of Who Your Real Friends Are

I suggested to Mary that she start practising taking care of and nurturing herself. By telling her this, I meant that it was necessary for her to learn that she had to put her own needs first, in other words to be more selfish with how she allocated her time. "Other people do it and get away with it, why not you?" I stated. At first, this seemed a monumental task to Mary, because when a Pleaser starts to please themselves it changes the relationship dynamics of the people around them.

Mary emailed to say how much she was enjoying the CD and was going to test out her new found confidence that evening with a 'drinking' friend. When Mary came in to see me the next week she was grumpy, angry and anxious. Mary explained why. "I told my friend that I only wanted to share one bottle of wine and then head home." She said her friend agreed: they all needed to cut back on their drinking and so one bottle of wine was purchased. After a while, the bottle was empty, and it was then that Mary's friend suggested they needed another. Mary said no and went to the toilet with plans of heading home. Mary was horrified to find, on her return, that her friend had purchased another bottle, egging her on that going home was boring as they were having such a great time.

In fact the truth was, Mary said, secretly she wasn't having a great time at all. She had sat most of the evening listening to her friend's problems. Mary came home feeling unloved, used and abused and her Healthy Confident Part was nowhere to be found, for when it voiced itself by requesting just one bottle of wine because that was all it wanted, it was silenced and then completely squashed by her friend. So Mary shared the other bottle of wine, even though she did not want to.

Pleasers are Free Therapists

Be careful: needy people love Pleaser people because they listen, they drink and they give free advice and often pay the bill, too. What a great set-up this is for many needy people!

I explained to Mary that we are often challenged by friends who pour out their own problems in the hope that the Pleaser will make them feel better and, of course, they do. It is very difficult for a Pleaser not to listen to other people's problems because they are usually good at advising and helping, and this is why they become free therapists to others, which can be exhausting and time-consuming.

Pleasing Yourself

When a person begins to work with their Pleaser it can have an interesting effect which could be likened to throwing a pebble into a lake, and through this action circles radiate out and relationship dynamics can change.

I suggested to Mary that she needed to crawl before she could walk and, at the time, staying away from that particular friend was her only option. I advised her to take baby steps and take them one at a time.

I felt I had to be tough with Mary, because if she didn't change her Pleaser habit immediately her over-drinking would become habitual and this would only lead her further on the one-way path to self-destruction that she was clearly already on. I posed the question to Mary: "How long are you going to keep saying yes to everyone? Will it be when you go bankrupt? Or perhaps have an emotional breakdown? Then let's see who is truly around for you."

White Lies

Mary agreed that she needed to avoid certain people for a while, which meant the 'little white lie' theory came into play. I don't like lies at the best of times, but for a Pleaser this is a must because they cannot say the word 'no'.

In order for Mary to build successful software of learning how to please her Healthy Confident Part, she told her friends a necessary 'white' lie: that due to unexpected work commitments she was going to have to lay off the alcohol as it had been noted at work that she was under-performing. People sympathised and Mary was on her way to building her Healthy Confident Part. Mary was counting her alcohol-free days (AFDs), and felt really proud of herself. Mary's Pleaser messaged the people she didn't want to see (Pleasers love text messages and answerphones). Mary was getting good at slowly but surely choosing who to spend time with and who not to. Her energy levels were higher and her concentration became better. Her boss even commented how much more assertive she was and this affirmed that her Healthy Confident Part was truly there and was becoming stronger, healthier and more present in her daily life.

Alcohol and Assertiveness

Pleasers, when socialising, need to over-drink because it means they can say things to people which they wouldn't say sober, and therefore they can often come across as angry too. Pleasers, due to their lack of assertiveness, will drink to express their real opinion. I believe this is another common reason for drinking. People drink to be assertive and say what they want to say; this is because the Pleaser, like the Inner Critic, suppresses itself when drinking and is replaced with childlike, sexy or defiant behaviour.

The Pleaser represents a deep rooted fear of not being liked which is once again suppressed by alcohol, and often 'fearful' discussions become more relaxed so the vicious cycle of drinking to express becomes an emotional habit.

Pleasers' Own Problems

Pleasers are not keen on expressing how they feel about their lives to other people. The Pleaser part finds this uncomfortable, because it thinks if other people know they are vulnerable then they may not be there to please them. Pleasers are always saying they are fine, and yet most of the time they are not. They are swimming in their own low self-esteem because they do not value themselves as much as other people. This low self-worth leads to moodiness and a sense of wanting to hibernate from the outside world. Pleasers need to retreat from time to time, simply to re-charge their batteries, and sleep is a way of achieving this.

Ill Health

Pleasers don't get sick very often; however, when they do, they do it well. Being ill is the only socially acceptable method of gaining attention or they tell a 'white' lie that they are not feeling well, which is then an acceptable way to get out of drinking. However, there is another side to this coin, for real illness can lead the Pleaser to feel guilty. When a Pleaser is ill this means they cannot look after other people and it makes them feel guilty because they need taking care of instead of taking care of others, so they avoid getting ill at any cost. They also can be hypochondriacs, always having a worse disease than you because in their unconscious mind this is their only perceived 'legal' way of accepting attention.

Illness can also be a safety mechanism to release the anxiety the Pleaser has physically stored in his or her body. Being ill is also a method of being able to get away and rest from the anxiety the Pleaser creates, so it is often used as a time out tool.

Mind Reader

The Pleaser part is often intuitive to other people's needs. Like the Inner Critic, the Pleaser also thinks it can read other people's minds and to a certain extent it can. The Pleaser has become so clever at picking up on other people's problems that they become the crystal ball reader, assuring people that everything is going to turn out alright for them.

On the other hand, over a period of time the Pleaser can become irritated with the fact that people cannot read their mind. This then stews and becomes a ball of anger because its voice is not being heard. This usually happens through a build-up of a long standing situation which leads the Pleaser to a complete outburst of rage, and when a Pleaser blows you don't want to be anywhere near because it's like Mount Etna! This form of outburst can also be successfully achieved by the Pleaser after too much alcohol is consumed.

Inability to Ask for Help

If you are a Pleaser, asking for help is generally a big issue. You are great at saying yes to everyone else, but opening up to your own problems and sharing them is unacceptable. This is because the Pleaser is worried that if people knew their fears and vulnerabilities they wouldn't want to hang around them, because they fear that these people will not be understanding and strong enough to help them with their own problems.

Friends and family get tired of asking if a Pleaser is alright because they always get the same answer: "I'm fine" even when they are not. So is it any wonder that after a while people stop asking a Pleaser how they are?

Pete's father died when he was 16 and he learnt very quickly to become the man of the house. In order to protect his mother he became the 'strong' one of the family and unconsciously decided that always being reliable, kind, honest and hardworking was essential to keep his mother safe. There is nothing wrong with being kind and honest and reliability is a necessity for healthy relationships; however, Pete took it to the maximum.

By the time Pete walked through my clinic door he was emotionally exhausted. His wife had insisted that he make an appointment to see me because he was so stressed and it became apparent to me that Pete had a very strong Pleaser personality.

Pleasers, as mentioned, don't like admitting their problems, and will often make jokes to hide their vulnerabilities – Pete was no exception.

Pete, a self-made millionaire, ran a company with 45 staff, had two children in private school and a mother in a very expensive nursing home. He was also on the board of three major companies and was one of the organisers of a local charity as well as being the coach of his son's football team. Pete was exhausted from juggling everyone in his life and it was clear that he was on the verge of dropping a few balls. In fact, I was exhausted just listening to him!

Pete clearly couldn't say no as his Pleaser worried incessantly that if he said no then he would be rejected, and this overriding fear only created more 'yes' and more stress.

Alcohol was Pete's way of alleviating the stress and this was causing problems at home. Pete drank to drown the demands of his Pleaser and in doing so was magnifying the problems with his wife.

I asked Pete: what was the one thing he could do to assert his Healthy Confident Part? This was daunting as he had never thought this was an option. Never underestimate the power of the Pleaser. It may seem weak by nature but it is a powerful part that can destroy the best of people and in Pete's case this was true.

In order for Pete to achieve some peace he needed to delegate, so I asked him to make a list of all the things he could hand over to someone else in his work place. He thought about this and replied that he knew he could hand over work to certain employees who would relish the idea of taking on more responsibility. Once again, the Baby Step programme was put in place.

The next week when Pete came to see me, he had managed two AFDs, which he said was unheard of for him. He listened to his CD when he got home from work rather than reaching for a drink and this was proving to be a routine he enjoyed. His wife also enjoyed seeing her husband more relaxed and delegating to his staff, which was giving them a sense of self-worth because he trusted them.

The Assertive Positive Pleaser

The Pleaser part has so much to offer. It has a genuine desire for kindness, warmth, fairness and unconditional love that can be used for you too. It just takes practice.

If you look at all the qualities the Pleaser has to offer everybody else, you can see for yourself what a wonderful asset it can be. Imagine if you started to nurture yourself. At this point you may experience a little bit of uneasy stirring inside you because the Pleaser is concerned that if you look after yourself then you will be rejected by other people. It is normal for a Pleaser to feel this way and I would be surprised if you didn't have any stirring. In fact, if you do not have any feelings of stirring, then congratulations – you do not have a strong Pleaser! Training your Pleaser to spend time out looking after you can be stressful and a little testing, to say the least, but the people you know will get used to it and you will, too. If someone doesn't like you saying no or taking time out then the relationship clearly is not a supportive one and you may need to change it anyway. This process is like starting a new relationship; however, this time it is with your self.

How the Pleaser Can Work With You Rather Than Against You

What a pleasure it is to still look after people with the knowledge that caring comes from your own choice rather than fear. The good news is that having a Pleaser personality means that you will always be interested in other people and the world around you. Pleasers love exploring new ideas because it aids them in their conversation and giving advice.

You Have a Choice

Being free to express what you want to say means that there is no mind reading going on. People are relieved when you say what you want because it makes it easier for them, not more difficult. It also means that you will be able to have healthier relationships with the people around you without having to get drunk to express yourself, and the beauty of this is that you will be able to achieve more because you have expressed to them what you want sober and that you mean business.

The alternative to not saying what you want to another person means you come home angry that somebody else has had their way, and there waiting is that glass of alcohol to push down your anger.

Having the freedom to be able to do what you want to do means you won't feel the need to push down your feelings through the use of alcohol, therefore you will feel more in control of your life. The domino effect of this experience will result in an increase in self-esteem and healthier relationships with the people around you.

Embrace your Inner Pleaser as a wonderful part that now knows it is safe to be a little selfish with your time and your energy, so you can develop the self-belief which will now positively enhance your life and future. Your world will blossom and so will you!

Something to Think About

Practise Privately

One of the best ways to introduce your assertive Pleaser part is to rehearse privately at home; for example, if you have a difficult relationship with your boss and perhaps you feel unable to say what you want to say. Start to rehearse just a little something that you have wanted to say to him for some time, without using alcohol. Remember to take baby steps: this way you will gradually gain confidence. The best time to do this is while listening to the CD. While listening to the CD use all of your senses. So the repetition is simply going to affirm and file in your software that pleasing yourself is a safe and normal experience. At home, or somewhere where you can simply be with yourself, go over and over in your mind what you want to say in a kind but definite way. Other people say what they want to say – why shouldn't you?

Chapter 8

Your Present and Your Future

Making Positive Changes in Your Present and Your Future

Reading through the previous chapters, you will have gained insight and understanding into how we are thinking, feeling and learning at all times, whether or not we are conscious of it. And it is with this in mind that we are now going to look at creating a more positive present and future that represents your Healthy Confident Part.

Every moment of your life, you have reacted in a particular way because your emotional software has filed past memories and brings these forward in certain situations, so you react in the same behaviour pattern. These filed memories also, unfortunately, represent your present and your future because there is no new information filed for you to use.

If you don't have particular information in your software then automatically your unconscious mind will find something similar about the situation you find yourself in, even if it is not appropriate and is detrimental to you.

Memories are all you have to support your present behaviour patterns until you learn to create some new and positive thought processes. This may sound like a broken record, but your mind does have the ability to create new thoughts and hypnosis is a great way to begin creating a positive way to behave and react in the future.

Your unconscious mind works uniquely with the software you have created through life experiences, and the aim of this chapter and the accompanying CD is to assist you in not returning to your old drinking patterns: rather, they will assist you in creating new positive and stronger memories in your emotional software so you can cope with life without over-drinking, both in your present and in your future. With the assistance of the book and CD you will learn how to build and file new emotional software that represents drinking less, both now and in the future. You will learn to develop in your unconscious mind a positive emotional tool which you can access at any given time, so you can live a healthier and happier life.

Being in the Present

I find it fascinating that we often think in the past or the future rather than the present. It is natural for us to aim for something in the future; however, spending time both living and thinking in the present is a valuable emotional asset. To live now and enjoy this moment is an experience to be appreciated.

My clientele comes from all walks of life, including the business district of London where men and women are often stressed out. These people come to see me for a range of issues, from stopping smoking through to insomnia. In fact, insomnia is a classic example for discussing the present, because not being able to sleep represents worrying about tomorrow or yesterday. It has nothing to do with the present moment.

Working with my clients, I encourage them to be more in the present through understanding how to practise being in the present and not focusing on what will happen next week or what happened last year. We all need a break from the constant measuring of where we've been and where we are going. It is about learning to just be, being suspended in whatever you are doing at the moment and not worrying about the future or regressing back into the past.

Another aspect you need to be careful of is that often people drink because they assume this is a way of being in the moment, where they can forget about the stress of today, yesterday and tomorrow. This can work for a brief period of time, but once again we need to be aware that this form of drinking does not alleviate the stress; it just suppresses it till the morning when you awake with a hangover too.

Being in the present means you can't think about the past or the future; you simply 'are' and this is a wonderful stress management tool in itself. By listening to the CD, you can start to appreciate and enjoy simply being rather than doing. If you are aware that you don't take enough time out for yourself or use alcohol as your time out, try, even once a week, to sit down and read an enjoyable book, or if you don't like reading then listen to enjoyable music. Taking time out is invaluable for your mental well-being. Walk to clear your mind: this does the trick for a lot of people and it is free and beneficial for the body as well as the mind. As you are walking, notice what is around you rather than what is in your head. Listen to the sounds, be aware of the feel of your feet contacting what you are walking on, and absorb the different smells. If you stop for coffee, enjoy the smell, taste and texture of the liquid. Get out of your head, enjoy the environment by being and doing in the moment, rather than focusing on the past or future. Do not feel guilty about taking time out for you, for it will help your stress levels and clear your mind.

For a lot of people, not focusing on the future all the time creates anxiety because it scares them. These people fear that they will lose hold of the controlling reins on their life and so they will not keep on track. They look ahead constantly, working on the next project or the next job and the consequence is they take on too much and in doing this become seriously stressed. The truth is, trying to do too much creates burnout and by practising 'time out' to be in the moment your mind will learn how to 'be', not just 'do'.

One of the many bonuses of listening to the CD is that it is a wonderful way to achieve the experience of being in the moment. As you listen, you can just drift away knowing that this is your special time out and you have chosen to pamper yourself by being in the present. I also do talk about the future on the CD; however, self-hypnosis is a great resource when it comes to practising being in the present, about taking one moment at a time. It's about enjoying each day as a separate experience. It's a great stress management tool in itself.

Taking Time Out From Drinking

The AFD, one alcohol-free day and night, means 24 hours without alcohol. Deciding when to have an AFD is entirely up to you and will depend on your choice of lifestyle; however, I cannot emphasis enough how powerful and beneficial an AFD is. These days are truly liberating, because your mind and body have the opportunity to release the toxins from alcohol while clearing your head and energising your body.

Taking time out from drinking means you are making a sober commitment to be with yourself rather than alcohol. The more AFDs you have, the more powerful the message is to your own unconscious mind that life without alcohol is both a rewarding and an emotionally safe experience.

AFDs in Your Imagination and Reality

Make a list of the things you can do that will encourage you to at least try one AFD in any given week. If you are a Pleaser, you need to avoid certain people because they are your drinking mates, or perhaps you need to be assertive when they urge you to have a drink by standing your ground and saying no. If you feel you have difficulty being assertive, here is a little pleaser tip: rehearse in your mind saying no to drinking before you go out, or listen to the CD so you can just drift away and bring in these thoughts so they become memories which will help you to say no. Thought creates reality. This is your mind and no-one else can store these memories and feelings for you. Visualise, feel, smell, taste and hear all of the images. Feel and use your internal energy in all of these creative thoughts. Remember: you have the right to be happy and this is the beginning of your imagination becoming reality. Rehearse over and over again. See, hear and say it in your mind to your expected audience, whether they be friends, work colleagues or family. Your mind is learning that this is the response you give to the outside world when you do not want to drink or when you want to drink less. Keep practising in your mind. Remember, you are learning and storing in your unconscious mind the emotional language of health and well-being.

As the unconscious mind doesn't know the difference between imagination and reality you will, by doing this automatically, be sending into your unconscious mind a real experience and it will take it on board as having already happened. The mind will then be driven by this desire because it thinks it is a normal way of thinking and it will work towards the goal of an AFD or drinking less.

I use this technique with my clients all the time. Taking someone through this technique helps them gain confidence and a belief in self, whether it is drinking less, gaining confidence or going for that job interview. The unconscious mind will take the information on board and will then utilise it as part of the routine of where you want to go in life. The unconscious mind is such a powerful tool – never underestimate what you can accomplish through its power. Thought does create reality and the more you imagine your future drinking in this way, the stronger the reality will become.

When creating an AFD situation think of what you are wearing, who is around you and what you are saying or doing. Please don't be squashed by negativity, which will sometimes creep in; just keep repeating the image over again, do not doubt yourself for you have the ability to do this. Use every quiet time when it is available, whether waiting for the printer or the washing machine to finish, utilise every part of your day and night to build on the two wonderful goals of an AFD or drinking less.

Each Day is a Separate Day

Changing your relationship with alcohol will increase your confidence and motivation to achieve other things in life. However, please don't try to run before you can walk. Sometimes things crop up and you may drink when you don't intend to or want to, and if this happens it is important that you do not berate yourself. This programme is about connecting your Inner Dialogue so it works in conjunction with your lifestyle. Your healthy drinking routine is your routine, not anybody else's, so just trust in the flow of daily life. Sometimes an AFD may not happen and this is OK, don't beat yourself up about it, for no-one is perfect – all you need to remember is that AFDs will become more and more comfortable for you in every respect. See each day as a separate drinking experience so if you drink on a pre-planned AFD you will not create and follow the Inner Critic's condemnation as it says: "Well, you've blown it – now you may as well drink for the rest of the week."

Each person is different, and taking one day at a time means that each week for you will be a different experience. It is important for you to remember that if you do have one heavy-duty wining and dining experience then you have the ability to stop the infection from spreading into any other day. It is simply all about gaining perspective so that one heavy session does not lead you back into your over-drinking pattern.

When you stop berating yourself emotionally about what, when and how you drink you are free to enjoy life, for alcohol has become less of an issue because you are looking after yourself emotionally and physically.

Fear of the Future

At any given time you are thinking thoughts that cause you to feel either good or not so good, in other words you feel either positive or negative. In order to be in alignment with your goal of cutting back on alcohol and feeling good about yourself, you need to become aware of what your emotional software represents to you.

Becoming aware of your automatic reactions means you are able to be the captain of your own ship rather than having your emotions set sail and just carry you along. You need to stand outside yourself to see whether your emotional response supports you or not.

Patricia worked as a personal assistant in a law firm and one evening I met her boss and his wife at a dinner party. They were both concerned about Patricia's health and thought she would benefit from seeing me. Her boss kindly said he would pay her fees as he knew by doing this that Patricia would not say no: both he and his wife were genuinely concerned for her health.

When Patricia walked into the room I smelt a wave of fresh alcohol which I took as a sign of her being nervous. Patricia, a single mother, was near breaking point. Her energy was heavy and negative and it felt like a black cloud. In fact, the presence of her fearful state was so powerful it almost bowled me over.

I briefly explained to Patricia what I did so as to alleviate any misconceptions about hypnosis to help her relax. Patricia then proceeded to discuss her life.

"I don't know why I get so moody at work but clearly it is a problem. I worry incessantly about everything, whether it is going to happen or not. I worry about what may be around the corner and fantasise about not being able to pay the mortgage and having the house repossessed, then I can't think logically and so I drink to alleviate the anxiety but it's only making it worse. I feel I can't escape myself. I worry about the future for myself and my children. I feel awful because I think my children are picking up on my worries as well as my boss, and now I am worried this is my last chance. I don't want to work this hard for the rest of my life. Everything seems to be getting worse rather than better."

I explained to Patricia that I could only be of help to those who were willing to help themselves and that her emotional software had trained itself to view her life both in the present and the future from the desperate, panicky state which she had just described to me.

Patricia's unconscious mind had created and stored imaginary bailiffs standing at her front door. This was not the case. As we now know, the unconscious mind doesn't understand the difference between reality and imagination and Patricia's imagination was working overtime.

The Crystal Ball Syndrome

We all, from time to time, create the negative 'Crystal Ball Syndrome'. The problem for Patricia was that her unconscious mind had trained itself to predict the future. And it had perfected this future planning to such an extent that I was concerned as it had the potential to become a self-fulfilling prophesy. In order for Patricia to move away from her fearful negative state, she needed to guide her unconscious mind to reduce these patterns of thought, for this part of her mind needed to increase the sensations of being more in the moment.

I explained the Crystal Ball Syndrome to Patricia and asked her whether she could see how much she was hurting herself and the people around her with her unfounded fears and anxiety. I asked her to write down what she felt on a scale of 1-10, 10 being the maximum of the emotion of fear that she was feeling and 1 representing no sensation of the emotion at all. Patricia's response was 9!

Patricia was worried about things which she truly could not predict, and in order for her to experience living more in the 'now' rather than in the future she needed to bring in her Inner Child part so that she could laugh more and not worry so much about the future. She had suppressed her Inner Child when she became a parent with all the responsibilities this entails. This is not uncommon and happens to many people. Because Patricia felt overburdened with responsibility and worried about the future, she had lost all sense of living in the now.

In Patricia's case, drinking did not bring out the Inner Child: rather, alcohol only served to fuel her negative dreaming about what the future held for her and her children, so the magic elixir of alcohol only enhanced her anxieties. No wonder she felt helpless and that she had nowhere to go.

An alcohol-free week – an AFW – was a must in Patricia's case and I knew that as her boss was paying her fees this would be enough for her to make the commitment.

Even though she agreed not to drink for the week, I asked Patricia to fill out the emotional diary. Her 'play work' or prescription was to listen to the CD. I stipulated that this was a must and that she had to listen morning and night, and more if possible. I knew sleeping would be difficult for her as she couldn't recall an AFD, let alone an AFW, since she was a teenager and when a person has not had these days off from alcohol the effect can be likened to giving up caffeine. The person can experience night sweats and vivid dreams, including nightmares, as the body is detoxifying.

The next week Patricia walked in with a smile that said a thousand words. She told me that her sleep for the first few nights was fitful but she had got through this ordeal by listening to her CD. Then Patricia added, "People are commenting how much nicer I am. An alcohol-free week was a challenge and I was so close to having a drink on a number of occasions but I stuck with it. The strange thing is that I'm not so worried about the future now. I do have my moments but I now see that the glass is actually half full rather than half empty."

I have to be honest — it took Patricia 3 months on the Baby Step programme to get where she wanted to be with her drinking. Her progress was more gradual than for other people; however, her Healthy Confident Part slowly but surely became more present in her daily life whether she was drinking or not which was the goal, and the future became a comfortable thought.

Building a Positive Future

The beauty of using your unconscious mind to build a healthier future is that the software is being upgraded each time you listen to the CD, follow the DOWO and have AFDs; each of these builds and strengthens your resolve collectively. Each of these experiences affirms positively that drinking less or not drinking at all is a safe and comfortable experience for you.

The aim of track 2 of the CD (which you can enjoy listening to now) is to enhance all that you have learnt and stored consciously and unconsciously. Your future thoughts will now represent positive achievements, not just with your relationship to alcohol but also your general well-being.

The Mind and Body Connection

Hugh came to see me with claustrophobia, which was causing him problems professionally and personally, much to his embarrassment. The reason for this was that he could not get into lifts and had difficulties getting onto a plane: in fact, the only way he would fly was with the help of 3 or 4 double scotches under his belt, and when he was at home he couldn't even close his toilet door. Any sort of anxiety, when not dealt with, can manifest itself in unpleasant ways. Hugh's office was based on the 10th floor of a building in the city of London and he joked that he was the fittest insurance broker in the business.

Physical sensations cannot be experienced unless they are signalled from the unconscious mind. In Hugh's case, the sensation of fear had become an automatic response. Just seeing a plane in the sky caused him anxiety and a desire to drink alcohol to alleviate the fear. Even as Hugh was telling me his story, his whole body language became tight, his skin went white and his voice started to shake.

How powerful the mind is, that it can instantly create that panic. Hugh was panicking while sitting in the clinic with me with not a plane or lift in sight!

We needed to change his whole mind/body connection so that the sensations of being in those places in his future would physically induce a state of calm and positive experiences without alcohol.

Listed on the following page is a range of responses that the unconscious mind signals to the physical body before, during and after certain situations, whether positive or negative:

Negative Emotions	Positive Emotions
Fear	Empowerment
Rage	Passion
Depression	Happiness
Blame	Independence
Worry	Calm
Doubt	Positivity
Disappointment	Trust
Frustration	Being in NOW
Pessimism	Optimism
Boredom	Action

Setting Positive Emotional Goals About Your Future

In order for you to set realistic goals about your improved healthy relationship with alcohol in your future, your mind needs to imagine the positive outcome first. If you feel fear, your mind will react with the fear response. If you feel happiness, your body will reflect joy.

Hugh recognised from the list above that fear was experienced when he saw or heard a plane in the sky and his body automatically created the physical response of fear. Hugh also recognised that he experienced depression sometimes, because his Inner Critic told him he was weak because he couldn't just get in a lift like everybody else. He blamed himself for his claustrophobia and worried incessantly about his problem. He became frequently frustrated and disappointed that he missed out on some lovely last minute holidays because he couldn't get on that flight. This led to pessimism and sometimes boredom, because he felt he was missing out on some exciting moments in life.

All of those words on the negative side of the list had been created in Hugh's unconscious mind as a habit and it induced the desire to drink. The aim of our work together was to create the positive side of the list so that Hugh's emotions of calm, confidence and safety were being educated in the emotional software of his unconscious mind and therefore to be experienced emotionally and physically before, during and after getting in a lift or a plane or entering a toilet.

Hugh listened to his CD every day religiously and the results were fantastic. He successfully trained his unconscious mind that his future experiences of being in an enclosed space felt safe now in the present, without alcohol, and as he thought he felt these feelings because his unconscious mind had filtered them through his entire body. The new software was in place! This is his reality now and it will continue to be into the future.

Self-Hypnosis for Your Future

The CD in the back of the book is self-hypnosis and by listening to track 2 you are building a positive future because your mind understands the positive words that reflect your Healthy Confident Part.

Practise, in the theatre of your own mind, positive moments that reflect health and well-being. Use all of the senses which we so often neglect. Ask yourself: What am I seeing? What do I hear? What is the taste? What is the smell? What am I touching? Keep being in touch with your senses while imagining the wonderful positive outcome over and over again.

"I KEEP TELLING MY UNCONSCIOUS MIND THAT I'M AN ENORMOUSLY ATTRACTIVE BILLIONAIRE. IT BELIEVES ME BUT THE GIRLS DON'T."

You are creating feelings of empowerment because you know now that you can imagine yourself in social situations while saying no to drinking too much or to drinking at all, for your mind is filtering this wonderful feeling throughout your entire body. You are now able to feel real passion in a sober state by practising what this feels like in your imagination. You can hear the happiness and see yourself feeling independent of alcohol and that this is starting to be experienced more and more. You will notice that you are feeling calmer, reacting more positively and trusting in your future and enjoying being in the now more and more. Optimism is active and you will notice this as you embrace your life with more confidence, while being sober and alert as you look forward to the future.

Bonus Track

The last track on the enclosed CD is for general relaxation and well-being. You can use this at any time; however, make sure that you are able to sit or lie down in a place where you will not be disturbed. Listen to this particular track when you feel tired or feel you want to escape life for 20 minutes or more, and enjoy it as part of your special stress management programme.

Something to Think About

You deserve to feel good about yourself. You deserve to achieve what you want. Your mind does too, but you have to provide the information before it knows how to do it. Trust in this process and trust your self. Remember, the past is the past. You are moving on from your past, through your present and into the future by the power of your own mind. This is your gift to your self. Enjoy it!

Bibliography, Further Reading and Resources

Georgia Foster can be contacted via her website:
www.georgiafoster.com or telephone UK local call rate 0845 660 4396.

If you would like to attend a workshop in your area, please contact Georgia via her website. If you have 12 or more people, Georgia or one of her trainers would be delighted to come to you. Depending on location, travel expenses may be included over and above the cost of the programme.

Georgia Foster is available for private consultations in Chiswick W4 and at The Wren Clinic in Monument EC3.

For nutritional support and advice, please contact Gillian Hamer at: The Wren Clinic, Idol Lane, London EC3R 5DD
www.wrenclinic.co.uk 020 7283 8908.

To purchase Biocare supplements mentioned in this book please log on to **www.georgiafoster.com** or call 0845 660 4396.

For a hypnotherapist in your area please contact the British Society of Clinical Hypnosis, **www.bsch.org.uk** 01262 403 103.

Alcohol Concern
www.alcoholconcern.org.uk

Alcohol Concern is a source of information on a wide range of alcohol-related issues. Alcohol Concern does not operate a helpline, nor provide actual services to individuals with alcohol problems. For further help and advice contact Drinkline, on 0800 917 82 82 (freephone). You could also try **www.howsyourdrink.org.uk** an online programme to help people identify if they have a problem, cut down and control their drinking.

Voice Dialogue books:
Stone, Hal and Sidra. Embracing Our Selves,
Nataraj Publishing, 1989

Stone, Hal and Sidra. Embracing the Inner Critic,
HarperSanFrancisco, 1993

Georgia's Publicist:
Sue Blake Media Relations
020 8891 2203/07966 538108
sue@sueblakemedia.co.uk

Georgia's TV Agent:
Elizabeth Ayto Laverack
Media Ambitions (Enterprises) Limited
Tel: +44 (0)20 8940 2222
elizabeth@mediaambitions.com
www.mediaambitions.com

For spiritual/life guidance, Hazel Oatey is an Energy/Crystal Practitioner. Hazel is available for private sessions and workshops around the UK. Contact her on 07957 162 103 or by email at hazeloatey@yahoo.com

"I attended one of Hazel's workshops after my marriage broke up. I was searching for answers about my life. I feel so much more grounded and at peace now. I am more trusting about the flow of my life and have found a deeper level of understanding about myself."
Andrea, 35

Steve Verity, Designer
020 7833 3355
steve@fever-design.co.uk
www.fever-design.co.uk

Simon Key, cartoonist can be contacted via email at simonkeyuk@hotmail.com